Local Color

Local Color

Don Thompson

Aldrich Press

© 2014 Don Thompson. All rights reserved. This material may not be reproduced in any form, published, reprinted, recorded, performed, broadcast, rewritten or redistributed without explicit permission of Don Thompson. All such actions are strictly prohibited by law.

ISBN 13: 978-0615954257

Cover photo: Corwin Thompson

Kelsay Books
Aldrich Press
24600 Mountain Avenue 35
Hemet, California 92544

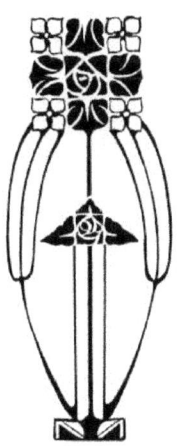

A lively understandable spirit
Once entertained you.
It will come again.
Be still.
Wait.

-Roethe

Contents

Night Watch	11
Reclamation	24
Wanderlust	41
Pilgrims	57
Beginners	75
Mishmash	91
True Crime	105
Empire	122
Morning	141

Notes

About the Author

Night Watch

Begin with this: an old metal desk
—property of Kern County—
scratched by moonlight from high windows,
the light I write by;
and an aching arthritic chair
with more to say
than I have
at three in the morning
when Time has nowhere to go.
So it stays.

(Audible non-tick of
the dead-stopped museum clock).

Sip coffee from a thermos,
strong and bitter,
brewed with a rusty nail in it,
not quite hot enough to burn my tongue,
but almost. Almost
alone in the dark that would be
frightened by the dark if it knew how.

(Non-click of retractile claws).

And listen to glass eyes plink
against skull bone,
muted by dust-colored fur:

The stuffed puma is out and about,
on the prowl, slipping down
from her soapbox in the mezzanine
where she non-howls all day at visitors—
silent, crackpot eco-rage against humankind.

She smells my blood.

Time smells my blood, too, and is hungrier,
more deadly
than any disintegrating mountain lion,
even with its actual teeth intact.

Across the room in a glass case
lit by ambient moon shimmer,
a kangaroo rat nibbling chaff
also hears the puma, but shrugs it off:
The dead seldom prey on the dead.

But here in this museum,
among artifacts of a picked-over past,
those who are alive do prey on the dead.
Haunt them anyhow.

Which some resent:
"I didn't come from cluttered St. Louis muck
to be bothered. People
are just sharp elbows to me, hacking
their way to the trough.
I ran free cattle in the foothills
up toward Granite Station;
kept to myself
with no bad habits to mention
except silence
that killed one woman
and drove off two others.
Neither worth looking for."

No name. Faint voice in the dark only.
But it's him, I suspect,
who hid the diamondback in my desk drawer,
its non-rattles clattering
like pebbles in a can.

"That's just like him."
A dry murmur from someone else,
but closer, the voice of
a woman who must have worn dresses
loosely stitched from calico flour sacks.
"Cruel jokes that could kill,
then the shrug and hard grin:
no-harm-meant.
Next time some unbearable tenderness
of gesture or touch—of remorse.
But never a word I didn't have to beg for."

Got that...
Odd to end up an old man, white hair
lucent with moonlight from high windows,
the light I write by,
taking unsworn depositions from the dead.

Silence again. Voices like smoke
from a fire burned down to cold ashes long ago,
thinning into their own disinterest.
And the cat, bored,
has finally gone back upstairs,
well-fed on something more substantial than
the gristle of my bad nerves...

Safe now to make my rounds,
armed with a six battery Mag-Lite,
turned off—
just in case the dark starts something.

Restroom first.
After too much coffee
for a septuagenarian bladder, relief—
if the prostate will ease its death grip.
All tile, binary black and white
(on-off, yes-no; now or never)
and porcelain older than I am
with drip stains from incontinent faucets
but still bright otherwise,
reflecting moonlight from a window
secured with steel mesh
to keep the outside world out.

I've seen moths run amok in the alfalfa,
a feast for white egrets—unhurried
because the supply seemed endless.
Here are a few under glass, rare specimens
of heartbreaking pale and dusty yellow,
so fragile they'd dissolve
if you breathed on them.

Dust is the local color.

Here's the only remaining locust
from a plague a hundred years ago,
harmless now
on its cotton bed in a little box.
I've never seen anything so alone.

But close by on a velvet killing field,
an entire tribe of butterflies
has been crucified for its faith
in the holiness of unrestrained pigmentation.

And the beetles, those warriors—
Samurai of rotten logs, night fighters
in the darkness beneath stone:
scarabs and unsightly ironclads,
elderberry longhorns,
and red-shouldered leaf beetles.
The drier and more brittle they become,
the more they glitter, translucent,
as if a tiny flame burned inside
each hollow carapace
as one burns in my dry, brittle, hollowed heart.

The last senescent grizzly in Kern County
went down in 1918
somewhere not far from Tehachapi.
Berry-smeared and bleary-eyed
with bits of meat rotting
under his trench knife claws,
he died hard
without a whiff of Verdun blood.

I think the museum had a grizzly once,
but sold it to raise funds.
At least the puma is still with us,
not pawned yet
(though a mixed blessing)
and two wolves in dead air
without even the wind to feed on.

The kit fox is self-sustaining,
nourished by her own diffidence,
her almost rabbit ears
listening for an excuse to be gone;
yet they continue to live among us,
urban, trembling
beside burrows dug in patches of bare dirt.

And the white owl,
too large to survive a lean season,
must be wired tight to his perch
or who knows
the mayhem he would imagine.

Don't try to tell me those eyes are glass.

A relief to wander among wildflowers,
even these mummies, emaciated and colorless,
that have suffered so much for so long—
crushed for our sins.

Old enough, I've witnessed the poppies
around Wheeler Ridge
spreading for miles and miles, dense
fields from a dream of paradise.
Gone.

Scraped from the land now, leaving only
a tentative orange haze on the hills in April
if we've had a wet winter;
but never tamed, never entirely broken
for human use like wild mustangs.

Some pressed, as if in a family Bible,
less flower than memory;
others dried to almost immortality—
instant dust if anyone touches them,
but otherwise enduring like dead bodies in ice.

And each flower with a paper gravestone,
a yellowing hand lettered card
with elegant calligraphy in rusted black ink
offering both common and Latin name
from the high church of science:

fiddleneck, phacelia, roadside thistle,
locoweed finally at peace with itself,
mustard, milkweed, mule fat,
the sapient gray sage (*Artemisia tridentata*),
owl's clover and Indian paintbrush,
larkspur, buckwheat, horsetail,
heavenly Mariposa lily,
and the lupines, somehow decadent,
suggesting *fin-de-siècle* lavender whips.

"My favorites."
The voice is too near to risk turning around.
Gracious, but aloof—a woman
who never had to open her own door
to any knock;
and then, as if finishing my thought:
"Nor my heart to any man's impositions…

"I grew lupines in my garden,
disdaining roses.
One could be eccentric in the nineties
with panache and enough money,
if one were indifferent to whispering.
And I could make anything bloom.
Except, perhaps, myself."

One more flower, a delicate thistle
with no common name
(though you always think of your first love)
and still vibrant in the moonlight,
its hues always changing,
depending on how you look at it,
from mulberry to cornflower to faded canary,
from ivory all the way back to carmine,
and impossibly glistening with non-dew.
In Latin called *Tempus Fugit.*

A light-bulb-behind-cellophane cook fire
burning tonight in the village tableau:
Someone forgot to unplug it.
I can hear the slotted tin wheel
of misfortune
creak as it turns slowly,
a bad illusion of flickering.

But enough where no moonlight reaches
to glow on the skin
of a nuclear family—surviving
manikins that might have immigrated here
from Weill's Department Store
when it closed after the '52 earthquake.

The unclothed, sexless child
with his or her supple stick and hoop
gazes somewhere over everyone's head,
listening to the sounds
I listen to.

Paint flakes from the mother's eyes.
A wig almost hides her indefinite breasts,
but she's wrapped in a modest,
moth-eaten rabbit fur skirt.

The man in an antelope loincloth
has suffered a chipped knee
that must be a wound from hunting Time,
so dangerous when cornered.
He's plaster white
beneath his buff surface.
A bow has been wired to his hand
like the owl to its perch.
Like this pencil feels wired to my hand.

Their house is too small for them,
made half-scale to fit into the space
of a department store window.
By contrast, the people seem larger than life,
already manikin slim, too tall and aquiline
for flat-faced and tightly-packed
Yokuts.

Who stood poles around the circumference
of a shallow pit,
lashed them together to form a cone,
then thatched it with tule reed matting
and sometimes smeared on a layer of mud
that dried hard,
sprouting grass in season
to bind everything together with roots
that, without soil,
had to hold tight to each other.

Primitive shelter, slapdash,
as much camouflaged burrow as dwelling,
though sufficiently waterproof
for this dry climate.
But consider the baskets on display,
all decorated—just because—
with rattlesnake diamonds,
quail in dark grasses,
steadfast little human figures.

Some to hold water,
woven with sixty stitches to the inch
by thick fingers in natural light.
And stout baskets
in which women took up their burdens,
more than a hundred pounds of acorns on their backs
suspended from a strap around their foreheads—
no migraines,
not even staggering.
Berry-gathering baskets like designer handbags.
And for fun, flat trays to gamble on,
tossing walnut shell dice hour after hour.

Just behind the glass
I tap on to make sure it's there,
a basket to hold rattlers for a shaman dance—
incantations against inevitable snakebite.
Last night the lid was on;
now it's not,
the opening a black hole in the dark
too deep for my flashlight…

But the missing non-snake
has made himself at home
here in my desk drawer, lying still,
content in a den as good as any other—
maybe better
than the basket he came from.

At this hour in this season of late summer,
the gibbous moon is briefly visible
through high windows,
casting the light I write by.

Write with a soft pencil, listening
to quill scratches in the dark
as if the dead were writing, too—
their own version.
Neither close to the truth,
which may be illusory,
nor to the facts, always suspect.

Bored by research, I invent
improv history; make found art
from bits and pieces
of the past's random detritus;
take what comes
like tossing walnut half shell dice
in an all night Yokut crapshoot.

"Your kind always plays fast and loose,
just looking for excuses
to avoid work, if you ask me."
A voice I've heard before,
an attitude I respect,
having been a retail clerk myself.
"Shiftless woolgathering
with nothing but words to show for it.
Pioneer Mercantile stocked thousands
of nuts and bolts, nails, clasps, and iron hinges—
all hard facts I could put my hands on."

And yet none of this is made up.
Simply an old man with a makedo memory
relocating himself exactly where he is,
exactly where he has always been—
where everything so surprisingly familiar
will always be new.

And something to do, anyhow,
on long watches
in this aging insomniac's museum
where no one ever retires
from sleeplessness,
but takes his job with him to the grave.

Not bad work, though, this night scribbling—
if you can tolerate
solitude in such crowded darkness,
if you can look into the black mirror
it holds up to your fears.

(Far off a hawk screech
like the ricochet of a tin bullet).

Endless non-sounds startle me.
Jolts to the shot nerves that prove
I'm alive
and not just preserved,
ruminating in formaldehyde moonlight.

And suspended overhead from thin wires
that sing faintly in the air conditioner breeze,
the sacred condor looks down—
motionless, but orbiting endlessly
somewhere above Time.
Hungry.

Reclamation

The rage of white water rejoicing
is first a thin trickle among ferns
high in the mountains;
no more than a hint of moisture
that seeps out from under the ice,
feels its way downhill, side slipping
in runnels that come together
like the loose threads
of an irresistible argument.

Even if anyone were listening,
the uncertain creek whispers inaudibly
under its breath, befuddled,
stunned by cold and only half awake,
trying to remember
like the details of a dream
the course it's taken every spring
for a thousand years.
Downhill.

(For water, gravity isn't physics,
but faith, the hand of God—
as Time is for us).

Gathers strength, collects other rivulets
and stumbles onto its first rocks,
familiar landmarks
—now it's all coming back—
then takes its first running leap
over a ledge and freefalls,
which is the joy of being earthbound water
with rain in its DNA.

And splashes into a quiet pool,
dammed temporarily behind brush—
to rest and recoup,
but also to increase by ceasing to exist.
Up here all the creeks become
one barbarian horde,
not Goths and Visigoths and Huns,
but the Kern River
assembling its forces to invade
the flatlands.

On downhill in a narrow gorge, churning,
the river finds its voice.
Close your eyes and listen:
you hear water crackle like wildfire
with the mountains throwing onto it
all of their debris.

The last, stubborn hold-out snow
melts in that fervor; run-off
from the shadows of evergreens
surrenders to the current.

Farther on, the river
has enough latitude to spread out
and slow down, to bivouac,
indulging its inner indolence—
also a barbaric trait.

Silt unwinds, relaxes,
and settles to the bottom.
Clear water, but deceptive—
deadly like all such pools in the Kern,
though sunlit trout hatchlings
flick like sparks, alive
and frantic for more life.

This is where the twisted road gave up
in my childhood, arriving,
after hours of nausea in the backseat
with my head out the window,
at Road's End Lodge.

Almost worth it.
No—actually well worth it

for the pine breath of a breeze
that knew how to talk incessantly
without imprecations;
that offered endless comfort
without one fretful word
or a hint of fear in its nightlong whispering.

And the battered cabins,
time-tested even back then,
were painted an indecipherable shade of green
that knew how to keep secrets
and kept them all
until the resort finally burned down.

Swimming there one summer,
I sliced my hand on a rock.
The scar is a second lifeline
across my palm, perhaps
adding to my allotted years.

Even farther downstream, the North Fork
and the South collide,
shoulder each other into a single channel
that rumbles out across a mountain valley—
pure force,
hoarding so much power
that it can afford to be merciful,
if not quite peaceful,
its tumbled music inviting us to the bank
to dance in the moonlight.

But not me.
Too clumsy to join in,
even alone (though not really alone)
here in the museum.
But I'll do the soft pencil shuffle,
my own moonlit dancing,
trying to keep time.

Trying to keep up with Time

because that valley is underwater now.
The U.S. Army holds the river back,
keeps it in a lake as if on a reservation,
contained. Almost.
Brimful, the packed earth dam would crumble,
so the Kern must be allowed to flow through,
some of it at least roiling downhill
along the spillways.

Earlier, Old Kernville gathered by the river
to sin, a congregation of storefronts,
saloons, hovels and hotels—a euphemism;
here and there a would-be actual house
overgrown with half-tame vines
behind its tottering fence.

Movie Street, dirt with boardwalks
(even in my childhood),
became a classic set for B westerns
with a hanging tree at one end
and a church at the other.
Its steeple and the hanged stunt man
looked down on Hopalong,
Tom Mix, Hoot Gibson, and the Duke.

Long since torn down, drowned, evacuated—
except for an old miner who hid,
was left behind,
and by the hardtack grit of his willpower
grew gills—they say—
and lived beyond his allotted years down there,
walking the lake bottom streets,
no more or less alone than ever.

"Nonsense.
No one ever said that."

My own voice, out loud,
without the added resonance of death,
sounds ghostly to me.

Now the moonlight shifts again,
drifts back to circa 1862,
illuminating the year of the trickle
among ferns high in the mountains
where we began.

No town then, just tents
and driftwood lean-tos without doors
(dark inside like the Yokuts' hut)—
improvised shelter for miners
who coughed all night in their uneasy sleep,
if and when they slept,
and woke with fever bright in their eyes,
unquenchably thirsty.

No alcohol allowed
up in Lovely's Big Blue diggings,
so someone laid boards across two barrels,
set out jugs and sold stiff jolts:
called it Whiskey Flat,
downhill close to the river
that never has understood human thirst
and passed by.

Passes by,

drops off all at once into a canyon—
not an ordinary riverbed eroding its course,
but a fault line, cracked earth
heaping up boulders;
tilted slabs sliced like butter
where spume explodes from granite,
the rapids refusing,
like Time,
to slow down for any impediment:

The river flings its metaphor in your face.

Heraclitus never saw water like this,
running amok, on a rampage, deadly
and too virulent for philosophers;
only seeming to pause
for contemplation
in a solipsistic pool
so that it might entice us
to swim.

"This isn't my haunt."
The voice has running water behind it—
unless a pipe broke in the restroom.
And has that clenched-teeth tenor
sing-song of the old gangster:
"We drove up from South Central one Sunday
to kick it by the river.
Beer and bud, a little this and that.
Muy pastoral.
But that woman, she crazy.
Strips naked and swims to the other side,
all dripping wet on the rocks, laughing,
daring me to come over."
Ripples of obscenity, musical.
"Half way across, a hand
reaches up and grabs my foot,
pulls me under.
A hand.
No pinche river could drown me,
but that one has more ghosts
than fish in it."

Another mile downhill, the last,
and the rubbled canyon walls
suddenly shear off into the San Joaquin.
Gravity no longer makes old testament demands,
but only suggestions
that the river accepts with a shrug
of quiet acquiescence.

Meanders among tule reeds,
revolves in eddies as if going nowhere,
but never stops feeling for
the absolute low point of the Valley—
the bottom of the bowl.

No hurry, though.
An old trout floating dead in the water,
its rainbow faded to a dull oil slick,
turns slowly into any current,
still traveling downstream,
going where Time goes.

The Kern is almost docile now…

Unless it's spring run-off before the dam
(and this is—circa 1862)
when the river in spate
slammed out onto the valley floor
loaded with upland cargo
of snow-snapped branches,
jumbled rubbish and mud,
tons of cold mud
slathering entire uprooted trees:
Men have dug wells here
and bored through redwoods
fifty feet down.

Primordial flooding—
a nuisance one year, catastrophic the next.

Yokuts knew how to go with the flow,
living dry on the high ground,
inland islands,
with their cache of autumn acorns
and fishing easily from reed boats
caulked with asphalt from a seep.

But white men, most of them
despising the Valley,
kept to the mountain towns,
gold or no gold—
Whiskey Flat, Keyesville,
and Havilah, soon the county seat.
A few, those post-neolithic dreamers,
had eyes lit with another fever:
farmland…

Christian Bohna is standing on his porch,
such as it is, looking out at the flood.
Sees the carcass of a doe float by
that wasn't quite quick enough
or just unlucky; a raccoon
caught in the roots of a dogwood,
oddly still flowering;
clouds of mosquitoes sizzling
with malarial fever.

A hawk, even more sullen in death,
drifts back and forth on the surface
as if pushed unconsciously
by someone deep in thought.
Bohna is thinking:

"If only we could drain this *verdammt* swamp.
But how?
With whose money?
Whose backs broken to do the work?"

But the water rises.
Ten acres of nondescript willow cleared by hand
to plant corn the hard way,
corn that clattered happily all summer,
tall and thick, yielding
one hundred bushels per acre
to load his cribs last fall:
Those fields have gone under now,
and the water seeping into the cribs

keeps rising toward his cabin,
such as it is—soft cottonwood logs
with a tule thatch roof
(a madhouse of skittering rats
since the flood),
no windows, no door
but a ragged flap of tent canvas
to hide the darkness inside.

Bohna's blacksmith fists clench
and hammer his thighs.
Dreams of a cash crop from fecund soil
sink in muck, turning to wet rot.
"Maybe no white man can survive after all
in this *Gott verlassen* place.
Time to sell out, move on.
Maybe try Oregon."

And soon he does have a buyer,
a crazier fantasist than he'll ever be.
Bohna decides to accept the offer—
two hundred dollars for what's left.
Which is nothing…

Across the room,
the kangaroo rat in its glass case
has reverted to taxidermy,
its non-life absorbed from it by
a man standing close in the shadows.

I can see from my desk
that he is breathing—
or pretending to,
inhaling the stale air I breathe
but exhaling dust.

Col. Thomas Baker has Poe's skull,
top heavy with uncombable stiff hair
scraped across it;
ferret edginess rather than Poe's despair
in his deep eyes, hidden
from the moon where he stands,
but fiercely bright anyhow:
This man makes his own autodidactic light.

"They call their lands after their own names."
He smiles, sort of,
with teeth as yellow-gray as ancient bone.

The fever sweating in his gaze
isn't for gold or land or even power,
but that most virulent infection:
the need to become the future,
to be the one unforgotten skeleton
beneath the chipped obelisk
in the old cemetery,
the bust with its authentic patina
outside city hall—
ignored a hundred years later
but still there.

(Men like that swim Time's white water
with the confidence of corks,
unsinkable).

Thirty years after the trappers,
a decade beyond gold,
Baker arrived here with law books,
surveyor's tools, no money,
and a second wife half his age
hard pressed to keep up.
No other intent
—ever—
than to create a town from swamp.
Which is also poetry.

Homeric, in fact, to contemplate
draining 400k acres of wetland—
displacing waterfowl, wild cats,
otherwise immoveable bear;
leaving fish to rot on the sand bars,
too many to eat; forcing
the massive bullfrogs into thinner
and thinner thickets of reeds,
their thumps sounding across plowed fields
where nothing answered.

Worse, uprooting
the root-colored indigenous people,
harmless but inconvenient,
even hiring some to do the work:
Digging canals they dug their own graves.

Reclamation.
But how?

Baker's head gate held the river
upstream, forced it
as scripture tells us only God can
to accept another course—
one according to human will,
picked and shoveled
by men with unimaginable patience;
and by the slow slip and grunt
of mules straining against plows
winged like insane iron birds
flying underground instead of through the air.

Later, land barons scaled up
to one ton plows
pulled by forty yoke of oxen,
gouging a ditch five feet deep;
that rough work finished by
Chinese labor dense in the excavations;
wiry young men, inconceivably far from home,
heaving baskets of earth
that might have snapped cables.
No one ever looked on
without comparing them to ants—
some ashamed to think so,
others amused.

Dug Baker's original ditch,
and then the Kern Island Canal
that still surfaces downtown
with its flotsam of miscellaneous ducks;
Poso Canal, Corn Camp and Deep Wells Ditches,
Goose Lake Canal, the Elk Grove Drain,
meandering Main Drain, and so on—dozens,

a neural net obsessed with
the Valley's never ending monomania:
water.

In my childhood, irrigation ditches
with diehard orange crayfish below the weirs
slithered along the margins
of postwar subdivisions, obsolete,
though not yet filled in
or sidetracked into buried pipes;
but all vanished by the late fifties
along with everything weed-rank
and too real.

"Remember the witch who lived
beyond the almond grove
in that house with black windows
and a crusted skin of dead vines?"

I do. But not the voice,
pre-pubescent Valley nasal.

"We were floating sticks
in the ditch, looked up
and saw her coming through the trees
with a .22 rifle over her shoulder,
hell in her eyes.
Quick to get home for dinner that day."

Who? A friend,
though not, I think, one of the drowned
we all knew who had ignored
—as we all did—
warnings to stay not only out of
but safely away from canals;
those whose bodies refused to dry,
lying there on the bank
turned to a bruised plum blue-black
as if the dead were actually another race.

And the Kern River?
Close enough to my desk at the museum
that I could hear it all night,
mumbling to itself
as it creeps through the reeds,
half stagnant, but determined
to reach that ancient lake bottom
where it can spread out shallow
and die in peace.

But you can't hear an empty river,
its water long since spoken for,
bickered over in courts and boardrooms,
smoke-filled once and smoke free now;
poured out in acre feet for a price
until dry:
a line in the sand everyone crosses every day…

The mad river made tractable at last.

Wanderlust

The priest looks out from his doghouse,
safe inside, but not intimidated
by the growling
traffic that runs circles around him.

Behind him and above, no-nonsense union men
wearing hard hats and fluorescent vestments,
jack hammers clattering,
work all day
to renovate the old Hwy 99 overpass,
having first built the plywood box
that shelters Fray Francisco Garces.

He stands tall, remote
in both Time and temperament,
twenty feet of unflustered limestone—
not aloof, not exactly,
but disconnected from our world;
ignoring us
as we ignore him,
although we have this in common:

The mandate to keep moving.

We rush to erase a few minutes
between outposts of everyday errands;
Garces dawdled
across a thousand miles of deserts and mountains;
often by himself, but not alone,
believing God had been there ahead of him:
Mojave was His wash pot;
the Holy Ghost had already cooled His heels
in every undiscovered river.

Upright now on his marble plinth,
no more than a mile from this museum,
his stone face lit by the full moon tonight
is all wrong.
The WPA sculptor (a Finn
less interested in research than I am)
gave him slightly milquetoast matinee idol
good looks with Bela Lugosi's hairline
rather than making him the lean hawk beak he was
with gray eyes like liquid nails.

Fierce. Fanatic. Indefatigable.

The statue's bland gaze faces south
along the main street of town,
looking toward the Grapevine,
less than fifty miles away,
where I5 tilts down into the Valley
and where, one afternoon,
two hundred odd years ago,

leather jacket soldiers rested under the oaks
eating grapes and telling lies.
Men with an eye for anything to steal
or an unattended woman—
but tough.

Their mules, offloaded,
grazed nearby in another world.
Now and then, someone would laugh
or fall silent, gazing downhill
through the obtuse V
of the shallow canyon's walls
to that immense valley below.
Endless—
you'd think looking across it:
like the ocean opening ahead of you
when a troop ship sets sail
from Spain.
(And in fact, the San Joaquin
is an ancient sea floor).

Haze and smoke drifted above the plain
(and still do, along with foul air
from the urban north),
concealing the mountains north and east,
the spine of hills to the west—
dry hills that crawled down into a marshy lake,
miles of shallow water
interrupted by islands
where the Yokut villages would be.

Don Pedro Fages, El Oso,
bear hunter with a grizzly's bad temper,
maintained command distance,
scratching his back on an oak
out of earshot of his bellyaching men.
Couldn't blame them:
he had complaints of his own.

Junipero Serra had gone to Mexico,
scheming against him—
more manipulative Jesuit than Franciscan,
an empire builder
who refused military control of *his* missions.
And Fages' imperious high-maintenance wife,
Eulalia, would crack him
quicker than combat.

But that was San Diego:
crystal wine glasses, candlelight,
and church politics;
here, only an unending valley
with nothing to say,
and a lake holding its breath.

No priests whose prayers honed stilettos
or monks in their cells
scraping crosses to a point
on the stone floor, making shanks
as prisoners have always done.

No cardinals with less of Christ's blood
on their red robes
than the blood of rivals done in
on their way up from mere priesthood.

No bishops who have long since made their bones.

Poison whispered in the confessional,
folding money vanished up a loose sleeve,
gold coins made a thin mattress lumpy.
Cash on the barrel head of an altar.
Where was the Lord in that?

But worse—
to have nothing for sale or trade:
uncorrupted, inflexible piety
like Serra's,
for whom gold was worthless
compared to brokering the bullion
of God's will.

His men would have noticed Oso's scowl
and exchanged heads-up glances:
The old bear's in one of his moods.

Cross-legged with a drawing board on his lap,
the expedition cartographer
hesitated and then asked,
"And what will you call that lake, sir?"

Fages exercised his explorer's perk of naming
without much imagination.
Though literate,
with more Latin than some priests,
he was literal and blunt;
had just designated their rest stop
La Cañada de las Uvas
because of its wild grape vines.
Looking down at the shallow expanse of
water shimmering in the distance,
his nerves calmed by it,
he shrugged and answered,
"Buena Vista."

And it was…

He's not there until the chair scrapes,
then materializes, his ghostliness
neither solid nor transparent,
like skim milk
with water added to thin it even more.
But makes himself less ectoplasmic
—intentionally, I suspect—
by wearing an unbuttoned Hawaiian shirt,
decorated with Joshua trees
rather than palms,
shorts, and the sandals he lived in.

"Up before matins, as usual, I see."
The priest grins, his teeth
the same off-putting color as Baker's,
as the puma's on the mezzanine—
as mine in the restroom mirror.

"Good morning, Padre."

He nods in response, lifts one hand
in unconscious blessing
while the other lays a deck of cards
on the desk. As usual.
Sometimes he wants to play a few hands;
others, just to pass the time.

"I never told you I saw you once."

The priest raises his eyebrows.
"So that's how I got into your head.
Where?"

"At the mission."

He nods. Pronounces its name fondly.
"Thirty miles off the highway,
back there in the dirt and weeds.
I had one of the original cells
beyond the off limits sign
facing the cactus garden and fountain—
a trickle green with algae,
but running.

"Walls thicker than an arm span,
clement year round.
And secluded—usually.
Tourist nuns were the worst nuisance:
'Oh, Father, do you remember
hearing our confessions
at the Convent of St. Whoseit?'
I'd tell them I was retired.
Done with it.
All I wanted was to get back to my cell,
watch the ball game on the tube,
and sip a few."

Tourist myself, I had snuck
past the off limits sign
and seen him in there, beer in hand,
a cigarette stuck in his lips,
and wearing what he has on tonight
while a crowd somewhere in another world
cheered for a homerun.

"Garces had an insatiable lust—
for wandering;
and that Pauline itch to take the Gospel
where it hadn't gone before.
No use to rat hole men like that
in a ho-hum parish
and let them be nibbled to death
by bickering ladies.
They'd go mad. I did.

"But rain forests can be claustrophobic,
snarls of creepers closing in;
and the cities are worse, thousands of
clinging hands like vines reaching for you.
Six months in Kinshasa
and they sent me home, a wreck.

"Which is why,"
the priest's chuckle rattles its dry pods,
"God created wide open spaces,
horizons you'll never catch up with—
that holy terra incognita
Francisco Garces needed.
And so do you."

"Wouldn't you call this museum oppressive—
and your cell?"

He pokes a milky finger at me.
"Yes, but could you live in LA
instead of the San Joaquin,
skittering back and forth on the freeways
like something with six legs?
Or negotiate Manhattan on your own,
stacked in box upon box
like beetles, calling each other human
without knowing what we mean,
if anything?

"Besides, you have endless elbow room
between your ears."
That chuckle again. "And how far
up into the foothills do you have to go
to see forever?"

"Unless there's haze or fog."

He sighs, fans the cards out on the desk,
face down. "Pick the Joker."
I turn over the ace of spades, of course.
"Wrong.
But you're missing the point:
There's no Joker in my deck, son,
only Christ and Him crucified."

"Amen, Padre."
Open a drawer for my own deck,
luckily not the one with a diamondback in it,
and we lay our cards out in silence
for Double Solitaire.

…Noon.
It's always noon in this country,
he thinks, hot enough,
even with perpetual haze or smoke
drifting from whatever happens to be on fire,
to suffice for penance.
Fray Francisco Garces is sitting
on a granite slab flat as a skillet,
sunlight spattering like grease
from the mica.

It burns, but his grimy robe helps,
bunched under him,
sweat-stiffened but indispensable
after a decade in the priesthood:
his second skin.
A robe so tattered and rank
that St. Francis himself could have worn it
without feeling an ex-fop's guilt.

Garces isn't praying,
though the Yokuts nearby suppose so,
but watching the current slide by
on a quiet stretch of
what he has named El Rio de San Felipe
and wondering why he's compelled
to cross every river he comes to.

"Why?
What do you think?"
A random voice in the dark;
and there are many—
some familiar, but others unknown,
like this thin and professorial
oboe rising from the silence
for its brief solo.

"I'd say Time."

"Of course you would."

That he won't have as much as he needs
to wander as far as he wants,
to unearth all the lost souls that live
almost underground
in huts like heaps of tule reeds
half-buried in the swamp.
You can't see them until you're on them
and the people, frightened
but inquisitive,
scramble out of the dark doorways.

"Maybe he guesses
—or God has hinted in a dream—
that he has only five years left."

Professor Oboe groans.

I ignore him, go on:
"So the river flows away from him
like Time: gone,
even as he sits watching.
Wasting it.

"And yet,
if the water is always changing,
if no one can step into the same current twice,
it remains essentially the same river,
which never changes."

"Heraclitus on the Kern?"

But in the non-chronology in which God exists,
there will always be enough
Time
for Garces, who gets to his feet now,
easily with animal grace,
and signals to the Yokuts
who lead the mules
zigzag down to the water's edge.
Wading across, they carry the priest—
a non-swimmer too smart
to risk drowning in that haunted river,
pulled under by ghosts.

One morning downstream, the sun
rising behind Bear Mountain
glitters like a halo.
Garces, on his knees facing east,
looks up from silent prayer,
chanting out loud:
In nominee Patris et Fille et Spiritus Sancti,
which the Yokuts gathered around approximate
for the fun of it.

He nods to his interpreter
who unloads from a mule
and unfurls a canvas banner,
choosing two children to hold it—
solemn and proud, then startled
by the image of a lady:
too pale for their world,
but beautiful nevertheless,
with blue robes and the golden sun
radiating behind her head.

Now the interpreter turns them around,
reveals to the crowd
a non-man painted berry-stain red,
horned with bear claw fingernails
and feet like a hawk.
White fangs, white eyes without pupils.

A gasp Garces expects.
He begins to preach in short phrases,
waits for the translator,
fascinated heads swiveling between them.
Finally offers a choice:
Virgin Mary? Good, they decide.
Devil? Bad.

Professor Oboe twitters from the dark,
"Nothing but a carnival sideshow spin
on Pascal's wager."

Where the Yokuts stand, on the bank
of a river at the end of Time,
the water is ankle deep and unhurried,
safe for once.
Garces wants to baptize everyone.
Some smile, some sneer,
some shrug and ask why not
like St. Phillip's Ethiopian eunuch,
kneeling in the water
while the priest scoops up handfuls
to pour glistening over black hair
that dries quickly in sunlight
already too hot for comfort…

Another time and place, another crowd
of Yokuts stood motionless, staring
not at crude, mission artist images,
but at Don Pedro Fages and his troops.
Those faces all looked alike to him,
varied only by expressions
of fear, rage, fascination,
or complete indifference—
which is the mask
we put on for oppressors.

Women wore short skirts
woven from grass and feathers;
men straddled antelope hide loin cloths
with domesticated aprons front and back.
All the same. Except—

"What about that one, sir?"

Fages studied the man:
skin burned even darker than the others,
hair blackened with grease and ashes;
he might have passed
for dark-eyed indigenous if not for
sharp, almost haggard features
and the panic
twitching across his shoulders.
A naked boy clung to his legs.

Fages turned to his interpreter.
"What do you think?"
Sullen, noncommittal,
a Yokut pressed for grunt labor
at a coastal mission,
he had tossed his long shirt the first day out,
reverting to breechclout, barefoot,
the only one of his men not trail-filthy
or foul-mouthed.
Fages expected him to vanish soon,
neophyte convert or not:
In his eyes
you saw an exile looking again at home.

At last, Fages said, softly,
"No Spaniards here."
A few tight-lipped mouths among his men
pulled down against the impulse
of a grin.
Then he raised his voice to a shouted command:
"Move out!"

They headed north, taking
no encumbering prisoners tied to a saddle,
nothing but trouble.
So let the deserters be; let them
wither away safe in their hiding places.
Don Pedro Fages had to keep moving.

Pilgrims

The new Ford truck caught fire on a whim
and burned the way Time burns
for an old man,
melting the (literally) plastic condo
next to its parking slot,
melting it like a Dali clock:

Faux New England urban renewal saltboxes
with vinyl picket fences
surrounding yards of astro-turf, no doubt,
too small to graze a pack mule on,
even if it were wild grass.

Oily smoke rose thick and black
from that ridiculous blaze
until wry firefighters stifled it—
and someone unnoticed
thinned and vanished like smoke himself,
who had been watching from
the dark doorway
of his solid doug-fir non-house
just down the street,
circa 1888.

Nothing plastic about that ghost.

Bones whittled from hardwood
with more knots than straight grain in it;
skin crazed like worn saddle leather.
Solemn. But unruly.
Mutton chops like gray moss.
And behind his eyes—
the wilderness,
more detailed than auto club maps.

This is Alexis Godey, pilgrim emeritus,
born anonymous in St. Louis,
who took to the hills with Bonneville at sixteen.
Fearless, quick to kill quickly
and take scalps with no qualms;
Kit Carson's sidekick, who conducted
John C. Fremont's brigade
along the equally unruly Rio Bravo
into the San Joaquin.

Later, too old for all that, Godey
became hotelier, beef broker, overseer
on Tejon Ranch—still breaking loose
to dance naked and painted with the Yokuts all night.
Divorced five times (literally); buried at last
by a fourteen year old bride—
no chica too much for him,
but finished off by the infected scratch
of a circus lion…

Now the moonlight seems dimmer
falling from the most distant and least
full moon of the year. And yet,
all the light there is comes down,
down through the high windows
as if through evergreens—
filtered, faltering, but sufficient
to write by.

No unasked for but welcome voices this hour,
although they'll come again:
not to haunt,
but to provide an old man
with harmless entertainment,
who might otherwise
have to hear accusations
in their four inch heels clicking
along the corridors of used-to-be,
or remorse in its scuffed suede shoes
with loose soles slapping.

A brief visit to the restroom,
bladder eased
and stiff joints uncricked a bit,
then back to the forest shadows,
the desktop desert,
armed with a soft pencil
for a black powder muzzle loader
and an eraser in place of
a Green River knife.

Lonesome out here.

But better than my own dark mind
brooding on its discontents
to imagine

Jedediah Smith, fundamentalist
misfit among hell-bent hell-raisers;
imagine him kneeling before God,
who bends a knee to no one else—
no one, neither white man
with a coin clenched in his teeth
nor bear-fat-greased savage.
Both perishing in their sins.

Who refuses to curse,
keeping his tongue dry as jerky
peppered by God's word;
denies himself the relief of obscenity,
that patois essential to Everyman
in the wild,
almost a survival skill.

Smith on his knees faces north this morning,
not east like Garces,
but into the opening San Joaquin,
listening to the wetlands
hallelujah all around him—

flippant meadowlarks like disinherited aristocrats
with no regrets,
and the glad chatter of birds in the grass
like tribal women at work together;
incessant insect noise, some hissing
and others clacking like the rosary beads
of those winebibbing priests
back at San Gabriel.

Gracious old world Spaniards,
but sly
like Smith and not buying
his babe-in-the-woods hokum—
how he and his men were lost,
wanting only to get home;
but they let him go
without their blessing
to plod north up the Valley
(just east of our town),
his mules impossibly loaded with
close to a ton of beaver pelt.

Teetotaler himself, blue-eyed six-footer,
Smith wore his hair long to hide
scars anyone would notice first—
not from vanity,
but to spare his neighbors the cold shudder
of seeing what grizzlies had done.

He'd fought back until the bear lost interest,
which they sometimes do; resisted
like a mouse in an eagle's grip,
a pitiful struggle,
while his men winced at a safe distance.

But survived with ribs cracked,
scalped, and one ear ripped off;
then sat still,
grim and stone sober,
for someone with unsanitary hands
to sew the pieces back together
with needle and thread.

Even God would have reached out
for the whiskey jug.

Born of New England puritan stock
(ancestors in country fifteen years
behind the Mayflower),
also inherited that westering trait:
Every generation of his particular Smiths
pushed the Atlantic farther behind,
pulled on by Pacific undertow.

Voices had called him like a prophet
from the Biddle edition
of Lewis and Clark's journals
—his second holy writ—
and Jed Smith took to the fur trade;
learned its craft quickly
and earned rank hand-to-hand
up the creek
against wicked Arikara;
then led men too rough for words
while keeping his own journals,
staid but accurate.
Owned the company in the end
and bought a dream house in St. Louis,
but died before he moved in.

Never without a Bible in his possibles bag,
Smith once spoke a eulogy
that forced tears
from men with hearts like old moccasins,
whose eyes had been boiled dry
in snake venom…

A dog barks, basso profundo in the dark,
a hound who answers, when it suits him,
to the name—

"Possible! Come on, lad."

The voice is British with its aitches intact
and acerbic, but cheerful
as if soaked in bitter tea
with cream and sugar in it.
A dead last son
who finished out of the money,
too intractable to soldier,
too godless for even the Anglican cloth,
and weighted by an Oxford pass degree,
he sank to the bottom,
debauched,
and then surfaced in the fur trade.

His Russian wolfhound, not quite visible,
flows along at a lope
in its own fog, settling down
near the spindleshank legs of the Brit,
vague himself, and too pale
for the wilderness, forever untanned:
an Englishman with his madcap dog,
immune to the midday sun.

Eyes so sapphirine you'd have to look twice,
cropped blond hair beneath headgear
meant for the London streets,
and a pricey tailor's finest work
gone to tatters on his narrow back.
Even in the shadows, I can see
the scar on his face—
not like mauled Smith's disfigurement,
but long and thin and oddly elegant,
more like a mean streak.

"Emptied a bottle or three of claret
one night, with my cousin
and a few nuns from White Chapel,
and woke up at Ft. Vancouver
six months later with my head throbbing."

Whenever he laughs, and that's often,
you understand his nickname,
which is Meadowlark.

"Took ship south, bunking
on bundled pelts
and first got the musk of beaver on me.
You'll never wash that off,
once it's rubbed into your skin—
or want to.
Been trapping ever since,
but there's not much fur around here
that isn't motheaten, is there?

"Traded my silk cravat for a pup
with a Russian at Ft. Ross
who had yearnings for foofarow.
No bigger than a rabbit then,
but twice as fast,
unless he tripped over his own feet."

"Always a problem when we're young.
And Jed Smith?"

"I'd fallen in with renegade horse thieves
on the run from a mission, fascinating
but unsafe:
Fickle as ingénues, these indigens.
So when we came across that psalm singer
and led him down Tehachapi Pass,
I cut them loose and
travailed onward with Brother Smith.

"Never laughed. Dry as an old maid
with a brittle soul, but quick,
no fool, and the man you'd want
back-to-back in a bad fight.
Gone beaver too young, nonetheless."

The wolfhound whimpers on cue,
as if he'd been listening
and understood—
which dogs do in another world.

"Comanches crept up on him
at a waterhole,
perishing of thirst and careless;
then rode on into Santa Fe afterwards
wearing their tame faces
like stumblebums from the rez,
dying of a different thirst.
Pawned his pistols for whiskey money."

Meadowlark and his dog go around
in a slow dust devil of fog
that spreads out across the ceiling
and disappears. Now,
alone with ghostly names
that won't take shape
and wouldn't answer role call,
some of them, except
to nod and spit tobacco juice on the floor,
I'll settle for listing them,
a random, makeshift roster:

FREMONT, JOHN C.
Put Vegas on the map, a black dot
where pilgrims needed to stop
to recoup their losses;
and pinned down
dozens of other vagaries,
charting the uncharted West
that illiterate geniuses kept in their heads.

The Pathfinder had PR skills
fit for Washington's impenetrable wilderness,
a high-end flim-flam man
—some said—
who even stood for president
as a warm up act for Lincoln.

And had the right wife for it all,
eloping with
Senator Benton's underage Jessie.
Gorgeous, the girl
Percy Shelley should have been,
but tough as corset stays,
she became the first skirt to cross
the impossible Isthmus of Panama.
Could've broken more than fingernails down there.

Recalcitrant rather than politic
like the buckskin men
he was man enough to lead,
Fremont overreached and talked big
until a lean bull winter in the Rockies
made him eat his words,
along with his boots (literally).

Trekking south
through the fat cow San Joaquin,
he bivouacked one spring
beside the Kern,
spreading his bedroll
among the thick, aboriginal wildflowers
he gushed over in his journal.
Sensitive, I guess,
but vain and often thoughtless,
he once stiffed an old Yokut
who had a tip coming.

CARSON, CHRISTOPHER.
Kit passed this way at least twice,
early on as a boy, pilgrim
in the strict sense,
and then with Fremont's brigade
as a made man—
his rifle stock notched
and the beard grown in on that baby face,
but still somewhat to the south
of five foot five.

WALKER, JOSEPH REDDEFORD.
Appalachian Scots-Irish, which is,
by default,
the bloodline that always flowed west,
fighting whomever needed to be fought—
still unstaunched.

First Anglo to gape,
gob-smacked, down into Yosemite.
Imagine that. But now
you'd want to be the last holdout
not forced to look into that pit,
crowded and filthy as Lourdes,
infected with rat feces
and bureaucrats.

Found Walker Pass—not eponymous,
but named for him by Fremont,
who worried about such things as
fifteen minutes of immortality.
Joe had moved on, job done.

(No one believes, not really,
that blather about being-in-the-now;
about how the journey is
the destination—

a self-important snort in the dark
from, it must be Oboe—

no one caught in the achingly
slow motion grind of the long haul,
discarding heirlooms along the way,
winching conestogas up a rock face,
eating the horses,
gouging shallow graves for infants.

But a pass through the mountains
shortcuts all that. Reduce
the distance between here and there
and we arrive earlier
where life is waiting for us
to get on with it.
Show us a pass, as Walker did,
and you've given us—

"I know," the professor sneers,
"more Time.")

KERN, EDWARD M.
Slipped and fell in mapping the river
for Fremont, according to legend,
and nearly drowned by
his own name,
survived to ice up and starve in the Rockies
when the Pathfinder cracked,
lost his legendary panache,
and almost everyone died.
Bitter but alive, Kern went on
to shipwreck on the coast of Japan,
surviving even that.
His thick portfolio of watercolors
includes both Shoshone and Samurai.

And who is
PETER LEBECK
—Lebec, Leveque, Laback—
whose bones, exhumed by
fin de siècle picknickers,
lacked hands and feet—tidbits
for Ol' Ephraim, who crushed his ribs, too?
Who knows?
Among Hudson Bay's ubiquitous coureurs de bois
under command of Framboise?
Perhaps. Or a horse thief
on the lamb with the Chalifoux gang?
Could be. But look
at that slab of carved bark:

IHS
+
Peter Lebeck
Killed by a x Bear
Octr 17, 1837.

Slapdash, as if a knife could scribble,
the name backwards in raised letters:
the mirror image
has survived the oak's slow healing—
and Time's for once unsuccessful attempt
to obliterate.
Peter Lebec, whoever he used to be,
has become his own unforgotten name.

AUDUBON, JOHN WOODHOUSE.
By then, the land had been skinned
of beaver: untold tons of pelts
hauled to rendezvous by mule,
then on to St. Louis and turned into cash.
Herds of semi-domesticated cattle
stolen, stolen back,
and rustled again to auction
on the Santa Fe market,
where no one worried about sketchy provenance,
as well as horses that changed hands like women
with no brand but a dollar sign.

Money's only good in the cities, though,
so the trappers went home—
those whose bones weren't scattered
across the Mojave
or stashed under an oak tree.
Arthritic, bleary old eagle eyes
whose youth, throbbing like a wound
that had healed wrong,
kept them awake at night,
hobbled the streets, so ornery
not even alcohol could kill them—
men like Peg Leg Smith,
who'd amputated his own foot
with a dull knife, dying at last
in San Francisco
of old age and termite rot.

And yet, beaver survived in the tule marsh.
Wildlife rife and well-fed
still cram-packed the San Joaquin:
elk by the thousands, wolves
culling the weak and elderly
to make a decent living;
geese thicker on the ground
(literally) than subway commuters,
egrets feasting on clouds of yellow butterflies;
near-sighted grizzlies
you'd pray won't see you first.

All observed by Audubon,
the son,
a birdwatcher on fur trapper turf,
but nevertheless, a pilgrim,
just as far from home
and lonely as anyone else,
listening to the dissonant night herons.

Beginners

On some long nights such as tonight,
I slip away from my scribbling,
not to make the rounds
but to stand for awhile in the north room.
No exhibits, no unfriendly taxidermy
trying to come back to non-life,
but a space without purpose for now,
waiting until the museum board
finally makes up its mind.

Empty, except for throw rugs
of moonlit dust, and darker, too,
even with north windows wall to wall,
it used to be a demo room
with low bleacher seats facing a platform.
Back when schools could budget field trips,
yellow busses offloaded
a scruffy, elated, unruly, sharp-elbowed mob
to watch the local snake man
handle his nontoxic rattler,
or a mock blacksmith
with a cellophane fire in his forge
(borrowed from the Yokut tableau),
or docents costumed in calico bonnets
who churned buttermilk
only the bold willingly tasted,
or someone in faux buckskin
with a lasso like Will Rogers
giving the white man's spin on
how the West was won.

But only the Yokut woman obsesses me
who wove baskets
there in the quiet midmorning
while we sat still for it
—incredibly—
calmed by an inner peace
we sensed coming from her
beginner's mind
to soothe the bad nerves
third graders wouldn't have for thirty years.

And yet we felt it.

Not old, as you might expect,
she must have learned from a grandmother
that ancient craft
of intricate finger work with colored grasses
more fragile than the thread
gentile ladies once used for embroidery.

Still in her twenties, I'd guess,
comparing her with my teacher that year,
amazing Miss Trout,
whom I loved hopelessly for her throwing arm,
who could snatch an eraser from the chalk rail
without glancing up
from the story she was reading aloud
and hit a snickering kid in the head.

Skin of a color blending pollen and dust,
exquisite; crow black hair
pulled tight to her round face
and full lips that seemed not to need words
as we did with our constant sparrow chatter,
she silenced us
with luminous brown eyes
that gazed out at this distant world
from another, even farther away—

silent herself. No patter
like the irascible snake man,
who also baffled us with sleight-of-hand,
and no costume:
dressed like a fifties mom
doing housework in a plain frock from J.C. Penny's
but barefoot.
Blunt hands rather than a pianist's fingers,
but deft and weaving slowly without pause
like water flowing through tule reeds.

And her finished baskets
made of sienna and yellow ocher grasses
with zigzags and diamonds
of cinnamon and burnt umber
were true museum pieces
that I coveted to hide my treasures in:
talismanic pebbles, discarded keys
with nothing to lock or unlock but secrets,
a hawk feather, trinkets from cereal boxes.

So I stand in that empty room
practicing the patience she taught us
and wait; but the basket weaver
is a ghost who never manifests
outside my mind.
Unless it's a glow against the wall
where moonlight doesn't reach,
or a shimmering inside a shadow,
or that peripheral orb
that vanishes if I look at it…
Like Time…

Col. Baker has abandoned
Christian Bohna's tear down hovel
and built his own adobe
where Ellen can hang curtains
made on her sewing machine—
rare and unlikely, out of place,
but an undaunted assertion
of civilized life.

Soon Baker will sow, too,
ten acres of alfalfa—a field
for travelers' horses to graze gratis
while he entices them to stay,
offering cheap land here and now,
mostly above water,
and firm plans:
the river manipulated into ditches
and a growing town
—a city in time—

already laid out with transit and chain
by Baker himself, hands-on,
with extra wide streets,
letters one way and numbers the other
on a grid—plain, serious,
with no fanciful, daydreaming names
on aimless boulevards:

Bakersfield.

And also on high ground
a mile or so away as the crow would fly
if it could focus,
keeping its mind on business like Baker,
not distracted by something shiny or edible,
is Woilo,
a Yokut community since who knows when.
Amiable disorder with everything essential
(not much) scattered within reach;
plenty of fish to spear from tule rafts
or stun with narcotic plants
ground up and tossed on the water;
birds to net and acorns galore
within easy walking distance:
no need to move on
or move in on someone else
like the white men had done.
And no streets plotted in Woilo,
just footpaths worn into the earth's memory.
But change is coming.

Thirty years later, the Yokuts
hunkering down on the rez,
their village on a hill, deserted,
will be scraped level
and replaced by the Santa Fe station
with a Harvey House next door
where men unfolding new money can meet
decorous young husband-hunters on staff
and not have to take up with squaws
as the trappers had done
—by preference—
or make do with girls from the cribs…

Not every domestic dog is a cur
huddled in the dark,
hand shy and bewildered,
whimpering inaudibly. Most have
the knack for finding a soft spot to sleep
until the next bowl,
which they'll lick to a sheen, content.
A good enough life.
It would take more than a kick in the ribs
to turn them aboriginal again,
running crazy with a feral pack
out by Lake Buena Vista.

And not every coyote has read Rousseau
and lopes upright,
looking you in the eye until you look away.
Some skulk. Some
eat roadkill because it's easier
than the unpredictable hunt—
all those calories burned for nothing
and the skinny rabbit escaped.

Not every Yokut who odd-jobbed
in town—doing chores
or laundry for a white woman,
maybe looking after her children,
an ad hoc nanny—
worked half as hard as she did;
or went any hungrier
with a hoe chopping weeds for wages
than hunting hit and miss
with a cracked, hand-me-down bow.

Not every certifiably tame Yokut
stole the horses and went south,
his manhood restored.
Some did, but it's not that simple.
As if only factory hands,
office hacks, and bureaucrats
know hopeless drudgery
and only the noble, naked savage
breaking his teeth on the grit
in his bitter acorn bread,
is free. Maybe
none is more or less liberated—
more or less.

My chair creaks, mimicking
a freight wagon already a long haul from LA,
grinding by inches up Jawbone Canyon
with a load for Whiskey Flat.
Twelve mules, all morose, muttering
that they have no good reason to live,
and two men who did.

The first shot from a willow thicket
killed the skinner, who slid
from the nigh mule, jerk line in his hand
turning the pointers toward the cliff.
They refused, of course,
backing hard into the swing mules,
all of them tripped up, tangled in the chain,
and more irritated
than afraid.
The other teamster, who'd been walking alongside,
wondering if he ought to unhook the grease bucket
and swab those screeching axles,
was missed by a shot that splintered wood
next to his head,
and too far from his rifle on the seat,
ran into the brush and hid.
Walked into town a week later,
soaking his shredded feet in the Kern
before he said a word.
But everyone knew what had happened.
Again.

The bushwhackers, a dozen young thugs,
ignored the dead man's worthless scalp,
but added two rifles to their cache
along with the mules, one each,
and equal shares of
whatever freight appealed to them—
not the hammers, nails, and crosscut saws,
but ammunition, whiskey, molasses,
and white flour with no grit in it…

Sooner or later, someone malevolent
had to show up. Much too solid,
he pauses on the mezzanine stairs
(unconcerned about the puma)
and grimaces with the same yellow teeth
we all have here in the museum.
My breath—not his—clouds.
Eyes like .50 caliber lead balls
with no light in them; bald;
pocked skin like bleached lemon rind.
His black preacher's suit has faded
to charcoal, and his shirt
must have been boiled in lye soap
a thousand times to be so white
and yet so dull. No collar,
but a pearl stud in the top buttonhole—
a foppish touch that's all wrong.

"You've been to the Indian casinos.
Admit it."

"Of course. Who hasn't?"
My voice barely rises, a whisper
out of the pit of my throat
as if I'd fallen down a well.
"But how would you know?"

"Everything wicked you set before you,
I see—and no need to ask how:
I see it all looking out through your eyes."

He approximates a laugh.
No accent, no inflection or tone,
an imitation voice as if computer generated—
inhuman, but organic
rather than mechanical.

"I don't believe you."

"Then why do those neon abominations
disgust you? And the slop
from the buffet tubs almost gag you?
Why does your skin crawl
to see the stunned ennui,
hour after hour, of women your age
with credit cards attached to slot machines
by long umbilical flex cords?
Their eyes are so dead
someone ought to close the painted lids.
You loathe the sin like I do."

"No. It's just amusement usually.
And no more meaningless than scribbling all night.
What troubles me is—"

"The waste of Time.
And you loathe the sinners, too,
all those degenerate Diggers
wallowing in unearned whiskey money,
still living ramshackle on the rez
with broken down cars on blocks in the yard.
Drunk.
You would have ridden with me."

"Never."

Now he tosses something that clatters
and spins across the floor
into the moonlight:
a chunk of plaster, buff and white,
matching the wound
in the Yokut manikin's thigh.
Reaches into a coat pocket
for a slip of paper, unfolds it and reads:

"Cursed be he that keeps back
his sword from blood."

Then another slip from a different pocket:
"Their children also shall be dashed to pieces
before their eyes. Their houses
shall be spoiled, and their wives ravaged."

A third, his voice amping up, distorted:
"Happy shall he be who taketh and dasheth
their little ones against the stones."

I flick on my Mag Lite, pinning him to the wall,
but he steps back through it like a gauze curtain.

(I should have said something
stronger, should have stood up to him;
or at least argued context
for his deceitful use of scripture.
But what?

Not easy to count coup on hatred.
It's too shrewd and if stupid,
too hard-headed to hurt)…

Before that surviving teamster's feet healed,
the word had gone out
for blood.
Letters written to the closest light colonel,
answers received—all formal,
grammar checked, properly impersonal,
and frightened calls for help.
And troops had been detached for the work
of spilling that blood.

Only the dusty but presentable captain
arrived in full uniform
with a twelve pound howitzer and two dozen men,
who wore remnants, grungy and roughhewn,
a mix of urban Irish
and Appalachian riffraff
whose own options weren't much better
than the Indians' they fought
if forced to.

Local volunteers supplemented them,
those who could afford ammunition
and rode horses that wouldn't go skittish
when the shooting started.
And among them, inevitably, Pearl Stud
with a Sharps carbine upright on his thigh
and mounted on a gray mule.

They found their way by moonlight
to the North Fork of the Kern
where the South tumbled into it,
posted flankers across both branches
to cut off escape by water
(the Indians better swimmers than most of them)
and closed on the encampment
at two in the morning,
herding their prey into the dead end
where the rivers joined.
Trapped.

No women and little ones.
"Bucks looking for trouble," someone said,
"which they've found—and plenty of it."

Pearl Stud shouted, "Kill them all!
No sheep here to separate from goats.
Every last one is vile
in God's eyes—
not one who isn't."

But the captain called for Joe Chico,
who considered himself chief,
a dirt farmer cum politician,
wearing mismatched and threadbare pieces
of several suits—a court jester's motley,
but PC in his own eyes;
who had the instincts
of local movers and shakers, then and now.

And Chico indicated friends and family,
sparing everyone compliant,
everyone tame and well-adjusted,
and left to die
those who didn't owe him a favor
or didn't look at him
with an obvious bribe in their eyes.
And spared the boys, too, ten year olds
thin as reeds and trembling.

Pearl Stud objected.
"Young renegades already
and dangerous.
Why let them go free just because
they've done no harm—yet?"

But the captain shrugged and said,
"Beginners' luck,"
gesturing with his saber
toward the dark.
The chosen disappeared
quicker than you could cock a pistol.
Then the shooting began.

The killers whooped and danced,
painted with blood,
until sunrise.
No Father Garces kneeled facing east
to pray for them;
no Jed Smith restrained them
in the mercy and admonition
of the Lord; only
the victims' jug to swill from
for the taste of blood mixed with whiskey
and loathing for the dead,

who were shot up like signs on the road to Hell,
battered with rifle butts
until their eyes dangled by a thread
or skulls cracked open,
oozing the Weltanschaung inherited
from obsolete elders,
who'd have no tradition
to explain this,
no wise guy wisdom from Crow.
All dead, gutted by Bowie knives,
their glistening intestines looped in the trees,
festive from a distance.

Which the captain kept, not watching
the fun, but composing in his mind
phrases for his report:
how he regretted the slaughter,
but thought it necessary to set an example;
how some Indians had fought back,
bravely, with sticks and stones…
But fire power always has the last word.

Mishmash

Crickets pianissimo in a dark corner,
inaudible at first, gradually
insinuate themselves into consciousness
so that I've already been listening
—how long?—
before I even notice.
And then their rasp modulates
into an ivory clink that must be
mahjong tiles. Voices crescendo
behind their racket like a dissonant choir—
the clamor of Chinese women
caught up in the game, seething with
adrenalin and gossip.

The north room was empty and silent
less than an hour ago; now light
with shadows moving through it like smoke
spills under the door
and across the room almost to my desk.
Hot and noisy in there—*renao*,
that untranslatable sino-elation,
packed with little tables, each with four players
elbow to elbow slapping tiles
and dishing dirt,
melding pongs, kongs, thirteen orphans,
and happy together—
unlike those casino gamblers,
poker-faced and laconic,
a thousand miles apart
across the muted velvet tabletops.

Behind me now, more clatter
from the south end of the building
like hooves on a wooden bridge
repeating an erratic rhythm
as if recorded on a loop;
and then a cry, the exuberant,
extended vowels of vaqueros
—*ee-ai, ee-ai*;
while from the mezzanine,
a melancholy Norteño accordion
(meant to soothe the puma)
drifts across the high ceiling to meet
sad voices obviously enjoying their sorrow
that I recognize somehow
as the Basque gardeners
I heard singing old country songs in the bar
as we waited for a table one night
at the Woolgrowers.
And finally, amplified
by the tile surfaces of the restroom,
a skittering, intricate bop riff
on an alto non-sax.

A mishmash, a hodgepodge, a cacophony
that makes the perfect sense
madness always makes to itself—
as if I've been listening to
a lost composition by Charles Ives.
On and on until one by one
each element fades, leaving
only the original cricket,
pianissimo, then fainter than that.
Extinguished.

Or gone underground
into the apocryphal tunnels
where Chinatown used to be—
still down there, at least in sections
that survived the fire of '04
and the '52 quake,
holding up under tons of concrete
poured since then;
and Time.

Old buildings razed and replaced,
most of their basements
filled in or paved over cutting off access,
you'd have to happen onto an entrance
poking around where no one belongs—
maybe in a derelict storefront
where you discover a door
with no hinges or knob, nailed shut
and painted like the wall;
crowbar it open and find
wooden stairs stepping down
into the dark
and silence—
except for the creak as you descend
(or is that a blind albino cricket?)
with your Mag Lite beam
sweeping away the cobwebs of panic.

Does this museum have hidden stairs?
Lost in remodels and earthquake retrofits
or sealed on purpose—one of those
urban legend satanic cult cellars
we scoff at in public
but wonder about whenever someone prominent
comes off a bit too creepy.

But those Chinatown non-tunnels exist
—they must—
if only as connecting passages
between vanished buildings,
still there like phantom pains
in an amputated limb—
once shortcuts to the next door neighbor
since in summer heat
the cool basements were like front porches;
or escape routes
for pimps and highbinders in the know,
clever as rats in a maze
when the cops kicked in the door upstairs.

So you could, conceivably,
find a way down into another world
to breathe air out of the past,
almost tomb air, trapped below us
for a hundred fifty years.
Imagine no petro-effluvia in it,
but the dust of horse manure;
no burnt rubber odor, but lamp oil
still clinging to uncertain walls
that could fall in on you at any second.

To stumble over rubble,
broken chairs and empty picture frames,
scrambled scrap lumber,
a gambling den's safe, cracked,
and a ledger book
thicker than a family Bible,
not mildewed but bone dry,
its crumbling pages
crowded with minute ideograms.

You'd think a storm had blown
through those corridors,
but the only ill wind down there
is a breeze so hesitant
no instrument could measure it
and yet so relentless
that nothing has ever held back
its infinitely slow crawl…

Sometimes it happens (or not)
that a restless Say Yup kid,
too young for the original Gum Shan exodus,
signs on to build the railroad;
and after sixty days at sea
in a wallowing, keel-cracked hulk
with its sails in tatters like the Ming Dynasty,
arrives in California.
And lives through laying the SP tracks
up Tehachapi Grade—
the tunnel cave-ins, the powder charges
exploded by mistake, the waste
of men worked beyond what mules could bear.

Saves his earnings
and buys land south of town, buys more land,
hiring two crews to cultivate it
(one Chinese and one Mexican);
becomes a potato impresario
and survives far enough into another century
to raise offspring too restless to plow
and purchase a red Cadillac for his wife.

And it sometimes happens
that the son of an eminent cattle family,
in Cali since Portola,
escapes dead end retail clerking
for the Lazzarovich store in LA
because of weak lungs
and restlessness
to become a sheep man first,
who once herded an innumerable flock
from dry pasture to green Wyoming;
and later the majordomo
of Tejon Ranch,
looking the part with de rigueur bigote
and matinee idol chin.
Lives far enough into another century
to have a photo op with Herbert Hoover
and ride in Frontier Days parades,
a legend—not on horseback
but waving to the crowd
from a red Cadillac convertible…

Tiburcio Vasquez had bandito mystique
and other assets: English,
essential for social action poker
in which the race joker is always wild;
knew what journalists want to hear
and told them, quotable enough
to make east coast news;
played guitar, a charmer
with good genes and bad boy pheromones
that make some women tingle.

And Tiburcio had the panache
to sell autographed photos
from his jail window
to pay off the lawyers that let him hang.
But even Time was impressed,
reprieving his name from oblivion.

And had acolytes, too.
Five Tiburcio wannabes stole horses
and saddles from a livery stable
and galloped south
up the Tejon Pass toward the canyons
where no one ever found their hero
until a jealous husband snitched.
But a posse caught up at Gorman
(where everyone used to take a break
halfway to LA),
hauling them in shackles back to town.

Not for due process, though,
five years in San Quentin
only to parole and do it all again
as Vasquez had done.
A mob shouldered into the courthouse,
encouraged the Justice of the Peace
to take some of his sick leave,
chose their own judge and jury,
prosecutor and slapstick defense attorney
just to be fair.

The rope was already soaking
when the trial began
and a beam laid in the notches
of two tearless willows
above a plank balanced between a pair of barrels
(like the saloon at Whiskey Flat).
Next morning, citizens
emerged from hiding to find
the five, one of them only a boy
and all with Hispanic surnames:
Dangling stiffs with dew in their hair.

Los Californios grumbled in the cantinas,
insisted the lynching was racist;
someone lit a fire in the alley
behind the upscale Arlington Hotel.
But the Anglos said no—and proved it
two years later by lynching
the Yoakem brothers in their jail cell,
a pair of white high rollers who had the fix in…

Men whose names end up on road signs,
on subdivisions a hundred years later
(Tevis Ranch, Haggin Oaks, Truxtun Ave.),
men with acreage in six digits
and money in seven,
are usually men with imagination—
profit's wild-eyed poets who can see
Xanadu with banks instead of pleasure domes.

But Gen. Beale's camels sliced their feet
on Mojave shingle, nothing like the Sahara,
demanded barley, and lazed
like kept women nibbling bonbons.
Bad idea.

Early on, such men looked around
and thought: cotton country.
Good idea.
Yes, and the Chinese stoop labor
already on hand could harvest the crop.
Brilliant. But even the *New York Times*
saw fit to call them unfit
cotton pickers—recalcitrant troublemakers.

So recruiters ran ads in the South,
boxcarred Blacks to Memphis,
who signed contracts for wages
that undercut locals,
and imported entire families
sitting up all night in day coaches.

Some got off on the wrong side of the tracks
and disappeared—
accepting a free ride west
for a contract that was just words on paper
they couldn't read anyway.
Others stayed to drag their sacks
through stalks rather than boles:
At first, those men with smarts
were cotton illiterate
and had hard lessons to learn.

Later, more trainloads for low wages,
but with housing of some sort provided,
bags of groceries on the porch,
a loaner mule to get them started,
and fields white for harvest.

A Black man with a contract
could endure his year
without being share-cropped into penury,
then hire on at a dairy
or muck horse manure on the city streets
with a dark cloud of flies over his head—
or move up.
Could become the doctor's dignified butler,
could blacksmith or barber in his own shop;
open a block-long secondhand store
downtown on a corner
where Sears Roebuck would be
and wear a suit
no more or less rumpled
than any white entrepreneur's—

could tailor, in fact;
even open the nonpareil Teddy Bear Saloon
or at least play cornet
in a colored Gay 90s band
and meet the trains arriving from Memphis
with more contract pickers
"In the Good Old Summer Time."

And eventually buy a respectable little home
a few blocks from Millionaire's Row
(off limits to the Chinese)
so that his starched wife could stand tall
with her backbone like a West Point cadet's
and stare down
any cracker in this Butternut county.

All years before "Birth of a Nation"
packed them in at the Opera House
and decent bed sheets were ruined by eye holes;
years before the ghetto
out there on Cottonwood Road;
and even more years before that summer
I worked the nightshift
at a truck stop south of town on 99
and watched at 2a.m., queasy,
as the National Guard rolled by—
dozens of troop transports
and lowboys hauling huge tanks
that somehow looked bewildered:

Watts is still burning.

Someone's in the shadows—an unlikely
high school student from mid-fifties central California.
His skin, darker than the darkness,
stands out against it,
but I recognize him by his clothes:
high draped pants, razor creased
and snapped to suspenders just below the ribs;
always a fresh shirt, madly white;
two-tone glistening wing tips
and (yes) chrome sunglasses.
An alto non-sax hooked over his shoulder,
he croons:

"Your friend that played the bass for sure,
drove his daddy's Cadillac—
a yellow '53 Coupe DeVille, such a sweet ride
relaxing in the back seat
with you white boys
to chauffeur me around town.
In awe, my-my, because
I could blow them Bird tunes
my mama sang me in the crib."

And scats a few bars
of "Ornithology"
before he fades out, fades away,
blending back into the darkness,
the flash of those chrome sunglasses
becoming a glint on the glass
of a display case.

Among my secret heroes—
an already obsolete Black hipster kid
among lead-footed ghost boys
and luminous girls
in cashmere sweater sets and pencil skirts
with insubstantial Capezio slippers,
wearing a string of cultured pearls
snug around their throats
to keep them in check.

Tone deaf, still envious of musicians,
I've settled for second best
—I guess—
a jazz scribbler riffing on
snippets of history
like old songs not quite remembered…

Beyond the almond groves,
across the irrigation ditches
where we floated makeshift boats,
in the Chinese cemetery
the dead turned over in their own dust,
too far from home to rest easy.
No grass like Greenlawn,
so well-groomed with its onyx stepping stones
no one wants to step on
engraved with only the basic info
and a suitable cliché,
this was more of a vacant lot
and instead of markers,

No Dumping signs—ignored:
rubbish discarded in the open graves
of those whose bones
had been shipped back to Canton
in red barrels;
broken concrete, fences
torn down and scattered.
An attractive nuisance for neighborhood boys.

Had been chosen originally for high ground
and sloped sharply to the street,
an excellent drop for downhill racing
in our Radio Flyer wagons
(also red for death—
or at least daredevilry and adrenalin).
We'd tip over the edge
to rattle and jolt our living bones,
learning that hard things hurt.

Now and then, someone was interred there
while funds were raised, if possible,
to ship him home;
and incense burned in his ordinary name
downtown in the joss house
with its door padlocked to protect the gods,
otherwise guarded only by crickets,
from the godless *guailos*;
across the street from a Mexican restaurant
and not far from Godey's ghost's house
and from the vinyl condo
that melted one night, its black petro-smoke
nothing like the incense
that still burns in the old joss house.

True Crime

Chalifoux refuses to come clear, muttering
incomprehensible guttersnipe French
as he hovers, less ectoplasm
than a smudge on glass—
like a latent soul print visible
only when caught in forensic moonlight,
the light I write by.

Quebecois trapper out of Taos,
a wiry runt who shuffled with a limp
and spoke English thick as bear fat
only when he had to.
Illiterate in several languages,
Jean Baptiste couldn't spell his own name
or identify an inconvenient brand,
let alone produce
a bill of sale for horse flesh.
Men like that, hard to track on the ground,
never leave a paper trail.

But out and out outlaw?
It depends. He trapped
as long as the beaver lasted
and fur prices held out hope;
if not, took to the illicit horse trade—
a bit too readily.

Oozed charisma or told lies big enough
to attract and hold onto
a crew of close to one hundred men—
a true mishmash of frontier ethnicities
(French, Indian, Tex Mex, Anglo,
and Euro oddments)
including luminaries down on their luck
such as Bill Williams or Peg Leg Smith,
who sometimes rode with him.

Known as the Chauganosos
(whatever that means),
they sidled into California wearing grins
somewhere between sly and silly,
suspicious characters, but useful,
skilled and well-armed mercenaries
during coup season
when rival politicos were looking for
an excuse not to fight.

Mostly raided undefended missions,
then pushed their herd down through Grapevine Canyon
(where Peter Lebec went under, maybe),
on up the San Joaquin to graze and fatten,
and finally turned east across the desert
with 1500 head of other people's horses
stirring up a cloud like a dust storm.
Never made it to the stock market, though:
Thieving Indians cut his stolen herd down to nothing,
and Chalifoux staggered into Santa Fe
with bloody feet, flat broke.

Nevertheless, a solid citizen by Taos tests,
who once served as a juror,
but slept through the trial until shaken awake
to give his verdict
in his own patois that translates:
"Hang him. If he isn't guilty now,
he soon will be."
Married a local girl, got by
on a marginal farm
and left descendants all over the Southwest
with six variant spellings of Chalifoux…

Another man with a limp, John Mason,
walked like a crippled bulldog in a bad mood
and talked hot Copperhead.
Blue eyes that looked like he bought them
at a taxidermist's estate sale,
cheap glass. Reddish chin whiskers
and a scar across one cheek
left by a man he killed
in a knife fight
over gold, a tawdry woman,
or more likely, an insult to the South.

Not a man to mess with, virulent,
but easy to see coming and get off the street
with those rotted black teeth,
new boots, and a rank hat of coyote skin
with the tail erect in front.
Cut his long hair in a fade underneath
so he could stuff it up in his hat
to look short. No doubt
a clever disguise in his mind.

Demented, deceitful, and vain,
a backstabbing bushwhacker
who considered himself subtle as Coyote,
the Trickster, though in fact
impulsive as a rattlesnake
drunk on aguardiente.

With Jim Henry—aka Spotty McCaully,
tall and skinny by comparison,
a bramble-bearded hillbilly in bib overalls
who'd done time in San Quentin
and escaped lynching in the goldfields—
comprised the Mason-Henry gang,
which rode with Quantrill ambiguity:
Confederate guerillas or plain outlaws,
haters or looters—or both?

Crazed by Lincoln's reelection,
set out to assassinate Republicans at random.
Even tried to entice staunch Col. Baker
to set one up for the kill,
since the man was a political opponent.
Why not? Baker refused, resisting
the irrefutable logic of a half dozen six guns.
Also invaded the home out on the Kern River
of Union sheep man Philo Jewett,
who escaped through a window into the dark.
Killed his cook with a butcher knife.

But after the war, the fun went out of it,
and the gang fell apart,
each sulking off in his own direction.
Picked up one by one, drunk
and too talkative—
the parched nostalgia of blood thirst.
A posse cornered Jim Henry,
after someone snitched to save himself,
and spared California
the expense of lumber and a rope.

Mason lasted another year to the month
after Appomattox, a diehard
loyal to Bobbie Lee and a fast buck.
Finally, hiding out near Ft. Tejon
with another leftover rebel
with a price on his head,
cabin fever made them paranoid—
both maddened by caustic whiskey,
toothaches, celibacy,
and by the endless redline panic of living
on the run from the law,
from a bad gambler's long odds,
from Time.

Neither would risk sleep,
looking sideways at each other for days,
muttering niceties:
"Pass the salt if you please."
"Why of course, sir."
"Excellent beans, don't you think?"

At last, Mason lay down and covered up
with his boots on (another new pair?),
pulled his coyote hat down over his eyes,
not quite, and went for his pistol,
tangling it in the blanket just long enough
to be too late…

The law back then, and for years to come,
was mostly improvised and ad hoc—
or distant: a long hard ride
to fetch a tin badge with no gravitas.
Keyesville might summon cavalry
to butcher recalcitrant red meat,
but crime was local color, ubiquitous,
lived with like weevils in the flour.
You'd expect social devolution,
Neanderthal self-reliance,
dog fights over every bone of contention:
chaos. And yet, men organized,
held meetings with decorum
as if wretched tent camps in the mud
were New England villages—
chipper white houses, green shutters,
and brass eagle doorknockers
with two hundred years of patina
on their spread wings.

And Argonauts looked like the known world,
including London sneak thieves,
shopkeepers, Oxford-educated earls
barred from the House of Lords;
Germans with a theory, French with an idée fixe,
Russians with empty pockets and tears in their eyes;
and no-nonsense Chinese peasants.
All sorts, even lawyers, who knew from the get-go
where the real Mother Lode was,
and professors of jurisprudence
who'd scorned tenure for the lure of gold
and when the fever broke, convalesced
in politics.

Others went back to their old trades,
set up shops, hung out shingles,
or grew bok choy on unwanted wasteland.
Neanderthals published newspapers
and said whatever they wanted
on the reader's dime.
Some gambled for their daily bread,
using their knives, if necessary,
on anyone who reached for a slice.
Or hid among the sandstone cliffs
of Robbers' Roost to swoop down
on gold shipments for LA
creeping along the Cerro Gordo road.

(Men went west to escape, believing
they'd cast a new self from gold
—an idol—
and ended up becoming what they already were,
only more so.

"Wherever you go, there you are,"
says a voice in the dark, cynical,
a Neanderthal with ink-stained vowels.
"Any place.
Anywhere in Time.
Did you once imagine you could
scribble a new identity?")

Early town marshals let things slide,
if possible. Laws
were like the rumpled suits they wore—
tight in the crotch and baggy in the seat,
out at the knees and splotched
with gravy or tobacco juice,
worn with crushed fedoras and neckties
that advocated capital punishment.
Insane in midsummer San Joaquin,
but civilized—an ill-fitting
emulation of big cities back east.

Cowhands still rode into town
on Saturdays in 1900, lassoing
chairs off of front porches,
to dispose of their pay just as you'd expect.
Then roustabouts bounced in
from the oilfields, wanting a beer, a bath,
and someone to scrub their aching backs.

The *New York Sun* (and why should it care?)
once claimed Bakersfield had sixty saloons—
in a town with dirt streets extending
only a few blocks in any direction.
Had more brothels than that,
usually next door to a bar advertising
(in code) "Public Dancing";
and even more makeshift cribs
in dead end alleys or scattered
along footpaths that passed for side streets.

There had to be a dive called the Palace,
first brick building with a second story,
well-situated for target practice,
shattering windows in the bank on the corner.
Also the Owl Dance Hall, the Hermitage,
the Peerless, the Buffalo Brewing Co.,
and the Bird Cage, offering
stand up comedians and prizefights
along with hardboiled eggs, gratis.
The Chinese 5¢ Saloon in Jap Alley
and the Poppy, both seedy,
were alternately robbed and raided.

A good lawman knew what not to see,
what not to overlook.
Which pimpled punk to counsel
and which to escort to the city limits,
showing him a shotgun
and a baleful stare.
Some drunks ought to be locked up
and dried out; others,
pistol-whipped sober behind the jail.

A good lawman could walk on eggshells
and not get yolk on his shoes;
could talk tough with a grin, harmless,
or knock teeth out with a blackjack
and not stop grinning. Understood
that saloons and bordellos occupied fire hazards
owned by the men who owned everything
and collected sin's exorbitant rents;
knew that the city existed on stiff license fees
and knowing, could close someone down
or shuffle and nod and do nothing,
sweet-talking the temperance ladies.

A good lawman's ethics, by nature,
were too nuanced for Peter Singer.
He knew when to live and let live
and when to kill…

How far is China from Chinatown?
An immeasurable distance
that becomes memories the mind misplaces
among quotidian detritus
as the years pass. Or worse,
an essential trace element in the blood
gradually depleted as you wither
and grow your stringy gray beard.

Do you want to go home again?
It won't cost much
to ship a handful of ashes to Canton
in an old tea can.

Bones are pricier, of course.
But what if you want to stand on your feet
to see the wide Pearl River again,
listen to its slow, murmured welcome
and forget the Kern,
those blistering fast rapids that speak
only the white man's restless jabber?
How?

Money.
And the *fan qui* keep that like a secret.
Men in boiled shirts smoking cigars
bought too cheap from Chinese shops
exchange bank notes with such reverence
you'd think they were the writings of Confucius;
trade coins like magic amulets
that heal poverty.

But a poor man can work magic, too.
Lee, Wong, Zhang, Liu, Chen—
anyone with a name like that
has the grit to sift through the tailings
of an abandoned mine,
to sieve the gravel with coolie patience
and find gold—a flake
missed by men in a hurry to get rich
with eyes too big and round to focus on it:
less than a sliver of
fingernail pared from a golden Buddha.
Then move on to the next unclaimed claim.

(Photos Dad brought home from Kunming,
from the Flying Tiger airstrip,
show hundreds of peasants hunkered down
under their saucer hats, hammering
rocks down to smaller rocks,
small rocks to gravel, and if necessary,
chipping gravel into sand
fine enough to pour through an hour glass.
Men with a relationship to Time
we can't fathom).

So work for the money,
maddeningly slow, but Confucian:
'The man who moves a mountain
begins by carrying away small stones'.
Or gamble on
the everlasting, irrepressible numbers game—
now run by bureaucrats
as a legal flimflam, a shameless
tax on the poor
who go down to the corner market
to pay the electric bill
and come back to shower the roaches
with lottery ticket confetti.

Chinatown was proto-Vegas—
if you can imagine it without neon,
without scale models of the world's excess
and not smeared across half the Mojave desert,
but packed into a few blocks
of dark, dingy dead ends.

Cops would raid the gambler's den,
who'd bail out in an hour,
his draconian fines going straight to the city coffers.
The DA never bothered to prosecute: no one
would willingly translate in court
and face the highbinders.
They'd slit an informant's throat
and go home happy to watch their wives
count the money on the kitchen table
while the baby played on the floor,
using stacks of coins for building blocks.

So work and save your pittances
or gamble and stay one percentage point
ahead of the odds
and buy a steerage ticket to China
—someday, maybe—
or travel there every day, easily,
floating on a cloud of opium smoke.

The rumored entrance is in a dark alley,
inevitably, set back, the alcove adding
darkness to darkness.
The door consists of thick oak planks
fastened together and hinged with iron
rusty enough to reassure you
about how long it will take Time to get in.
A battering ram couldn't break it down,
even if cops on-the-take wanted to;
but with the correct, light-knuckled rhythmic knock,
it opens by itself
onto a stairway down to a cellar.

And when your eyes become accustomed
to the red non-light,
you seem to be in the catacombs—
not Christian graves, though,
not with that devil painted on the wall.
The non-living, if not exactly dead
(a few *guailos* among the celestials—
and is that a white woman?)
lie back in oblivion drawing on long pipes
like silent flutes
held just above flickering oil lamps.
Someone is scratching an *er hu*.
Smoke rises and spreads across the low ceiling
like the breath of a burned out dragon.

Drugs, gambling, prostitution
like blood in the water
attract those lean, look-alike sharks,
not circling, but processing single file
and soft-footed along 22nd St.
in pleated black robes with a white silk sash:
hatchet men from the tongs.

Check their queues.
If swinging freely behind like thick ropes,
go about your business;
but if wrapped around their heads,
you've blundered into a gang fight,
so run. No shame.

And if a pair of *boo how doy*
shuffle into your shop one afternoon,
bending over the cigars
to inhale the fragrance, innocent
as nuns among wildflowers,
offer them a box
(neither the best nor worst)
with something from the till tucked in;
and thank them, sincerely,
for taking such care to protect you…

And there at the corner of 22nd and L
in Col. Baker's orderly civic grid,
stood a joss house—
not a tool shed in which to store the gods
like the temple a few blocks away,
but a multi-purpose hall:
an altar in a closet, yes,
but also warm beer on tap
bad enough to make you think twice;
gambling in a locked back room
with a hatchet man sitting outside
feigning indifference,
smoking roll-your-owns and reading the news
(six months old from Canton);
an opium cellar somewhere on the premises;
rooms to rent upstairs
with sparse, secondhand furniture
and hand-me-down girls by request.

On Sunday morning a week after Easter, 1903,
Jim McKinney had taken one of the rooms
and stopped running from the law.
Vile, venomous, vicious,
a spree killer and a sick prankster
who gunned men in the gluteus for a joke
as if swatting them with a gym towel;
who once shot the piano player;
who even performed
an impromptu partial mastectomy
on a woman who dissed him.

No secret that he was in town.
Was Jim finally tired of it all?
Or arrogant, considering himself bullet proof,
too smart for the cops?
Or had every thought dissolved in alcohol
and left him addled, unconcerned,
nonhuman—a rattlesnake
functioning entirely with the R brain?

He and his sidekick Al
and a hooker named Jennie (who ducked)
greeted the ten man posse at the front door.
A stunned pause, then shotguns barked
and Winchester dogs yapped madly,
splattered blood, cracked bones,
pierced necks and kidneys—killing:
McKinney fought hard,
but ultimately took two barrels of buckshot
that fragmented his thick skull.

The town marshal died of his wounds a day later;
his part-time deputy had been killed
by the first shot.

Perhaps the last Wild West gunfight.

And it was left to the son of the slain deputy
to atone for frontier primitivism
by singing opera at the Met—
a dapper man with an RAF mustache
and a baritone pure as cathedral bells.

Empire

Last summer's corn laid up in the crib,
Christian Bohna planted again, a man
alone with uncertainties
about rain or no rain or flood waters
churning out of the canyon,
about crows and rodents and stray Yokuts.
With no horse for them to steal, no plow,
Bohna covered his knoll step by step
with a sharp stick and a bag of seed.

If all went well or anywhere close to it
—but it didn't—
his two acres of scant corn could have become
160 of wheat on dry land
reclaimed from the marshes, his solitary,
painful labor taken on by four horses—
the measure of success for
a subsistence farmer.

But washed out, he sold to Col. Baker,
who had some money, though not much,
and sowed ten acres of alfalfa,
mostly for PR.
Had horses, too, and hired
lay about Yokuts to do the work,
whom he watched from somewhere far off
in his irrepressible dreams
as they broadcast seed
from the back of an aching wagon.

Only ten years later on fields south of town,
men with San Francisco capital
and dreams scaled up to visions
of grandeur,
could sow 1500 acres of winter wheat.
Chinese labor. Mules
weighing in at a ton and a half
bred from imported mares
(huge Percherons with haunches like Behemoth)
in teams of twenty with jerk line harnesses
more complex than electronic circuitry.

And no more plows improvised
from forked trees,
an iron share bolted to a root
and dragged at a slow stagger
by one horse praying to go lame.
But plows forged at an ironworks in Stockton,
three on a beam with wheels,
depth and width settings, angle adjustments
to prevent clogging.
And no more broken branches for harrows
to cover seed broadcast helter-skelter by hand:
now machines scattered it evenly,
followed by disc cultivators twenty feet wide.
A long way already from Bohna
alone with a hoe, a stick,
and a bag slung over his throbbing shoulder.

And then the steam tractor
chuffed into town, so amazing to see
that men laughed, women stepped back,
little children wet themselves from awe,
and newspaper prose turned purple.
Slow, but dauntless, unstoppable
once its immense cleated wheels got a grip,
its limits were never tested.
By what?
Could pull a train of wagons
with a forty ton load, pull it uphill.
And if it couldn't turn on a dime,
it pivoted neatly
around a twenty dollar gold coin.

Not so much a land-roving locomotive
as a steampunk elephant
with a serious-minded mahout,
who manipulated wheels and levers
and kept an eye on the gauges
while dressed in a three-piece suit
under a dusty bowler hat—
a man of his time.

And the tractor drank water like an elephant,
consuming hundreds of gallons at a gulp
to convert clouds of steam
into mammoth power.

Water.

Without it, not even money mattered.
And monied men went to war for it—
not bar brawls and gun fights anymore,
but torts contested by lawyers with rhetoric
like knives hidden in their boots.
Dangerous when cornered in a courtroom.

Haggin, half Turk sultan of finance,
whose name showed up on the letterheads
of Wells Fargo, no less,
and the Anaconda copper mines of Montana,
diverted the Kern River
—a cheap trick—
into his own canal system.
Left Miller and Lux with a dribble,
whose own holdings, if shaded in,
cast a shadow across the map of California;
who drove cattle from Arizona to Oregon
camping every night on their own land.
Lux v. Haggin
almost bankrupted both titans,
forcing them to settle, ultimately,
according to the riparian precedents
of English common law.

But not all irrigation water came from the river.
Deep wells provided for generations
and sometimes Artesian gushers
burst from the earth and flowed compliantly
into webs of shallow ditches.

I used to lie across concrete pipes
and thrust my head into the cold boil,
drinking water from the source
without a middleman
bottling it in tissue-thin plastic.

(Somewhere Saroyan writes about
San Joaquin water. I remember
gulping it from a hose like he did
on summer afternoons, sweating
from all that boyhood busyness in the sun,
ignoring the heat, but thirsty—
perfectly thirsty and letting the hose
soak my head before taking in
more than I could hold.

Now the chlorinated water may be potable
to the health department,
but no one wants to drink from the tap.
And garden hoses can kill you
with lead traces in the fittings
and toxic chemicals.
The whole world has become carcinogenic)…

Coming back from the restroom (again)
with its either-or tile floor and no-exit window,
I find my desk commandeered by
a big man, waiting for me
as if I'd been called on the carpet.

"Sit."
His voice, pitched low but crisp,
has no waste of time in it,
no attempt to simulate bonhomie,
and no needless effort to convey dominance
by insinuation or inflection.
All business.
I sit.

The dove gray suit fits like skin on a sausage.
Ball bearing eyes.
A fringe of hair like a Roman crown
woven of steel wire
perches on his baby-smooth skull.
Clean-shaven within the hour,
his pink complexion glistens, redolent
of a sycophantic, full-service barber shop.
The silk tie reflects light
like flowing water, fixed with a stick pin
formed from a gold nugget, unshaped,
just as it came from a mountain stream.
A crystal ash tray on the desk
must weigh twenty pounds;
beside it lies a sterling silver case
(no cigar in sight)
engraved with the initials RB
in florid, convoluted Rococo.
He notices me trying to decipher it.

"Generic," he says.

"But elegant. And expensive."

"Sarcasm duly noted.
Had it made for me by a Florentine silversmith
while touring—sarcastic like you
about the ancient rubble and one-armed statues
everyone idolizes.
My wife brought one home
along with a worthless baronet,
a fop for her daughter.
But this is quality workmanship,
and you can be sure its value appreciated."

"Your great grandson probably pawned it
for drug money."

"Perhaps. It's just an object after all, isn't it,
that facilitates a bad habit?
And you're thinking—"

"You could do without things like that
and pay your workers more."

"Yes. The workers."

"Where would you be without them?"

"And without me, where would they be?"

"I don't know, but they'd have
all their fingers, and their lungs
wouldn't be seared by caustic substances;
and their children wouldn't have to drink
water that burns like kerosene."

"Ethical anachronism.
No one knew the dangers back then."

"Of exposed machinery?"

RB sighs. Quiet for a moment,
out of arguments, perhaps, but unconvinced.
"They got paid."

"Not much."

"Enough that some of them
became some of us—
saved, invested, invented,
made a success of themselves.
That wouldn't be possible without me.
Besides, where do you think
I came from?"

"Here we go."

"Apprenticed to a cobbler at eight.
I could still repair your shoes
better than anyone in town."

"But not your own Spanish leather.
No soles worn through on those button-tops,
buffed to a squinting glare
by a Black man
pop-popping his cloth and grinning
while you perch above him on a throne,
keeping tabs on Wall Street
in the morning paper."

"He has a job.
And does his work with savoir faire,
not slavishness.
Would you rather have him on the dole?"

Now I sigh, stymied.
"But do you really require
a private railroad car
tricked out for a spendthrift sheik?"

"Why not? I've earned it.
I suppose you'd prefer socialism.
Tell me about your friend
who taught English in China
when the comrades still wore Mao suits."

"Isn't that after your time?"

"Anything in your head is in mine, too."

(I can't argue about
bicycles thick on the streets,
blown back and forth like fallen leaves
in a shifting wind called politics;
and no one in cars then
except the Party fat cats
curled up in the curtained back seat
of black Russian knock-offs
of post-war Hudsons.

He'd pedal past chalk outlines
of pedestrians they ran over
and swerve to miss the battered old trucks,
gagging on their fumes.
Everything built with concrete and crumbling
before it was finished.
Half dead trees coated with cement dust).

"And you want that here.
Rather than our system, such as it is?"

"Neither," I say—last word,
having nothing better to suggest,
no blessed solution.

RB grins, almost sympathetically,
snaps open the cigar case
without bothering to offer me one,
and lights up with a wooden match.
Smoke that ought to rise
thickens around him and hangs in the air.
When it drifts away, at last,
he's gone…

Huntington. Hopkins. Crocker. Stanford.
Not shopkeepers, perhaps, but merchant class
rather than scions
of old, east coast, evergreen money;
California thistles sticking to any loose cash
that blew their way.

Knew the unconcealed secret, the obvious
mystery so many others never penetrated:
that it's quicker and easier
to extract gold from men's pockets
than from the earth.

Mark Hopkins, grocer and bean counter,
wait-a-minute realist
balancing Collis Huntington's bluster;
avuncular, always troubled by
his partners' sharp practices,
but when swindle came to scandal,
Uncle Mark cooked the books
—literally—
until they caught fire and burned.

Collis, grease man in Washington,
picklock who cracked the tax coffers,
both blowhard and Jesuitical lobbyist;
first to contract transcontinental fever
from Crazy Ted Judah, romanticist,
who conceived a coast to coast railroad;
who surveyed Donner Pass
and laid it all out, doable,
on a ninety foot scale map.

Chas Crocker made it happen on the ground,
indispensable and ruthless,
always on task with no other agenda
than getting the job done.
Had the insight to hire Chinese labor
despite wrinkled noses:

A race that built the Great Wall,
he said, could lay tracks
across the snowbound Sierra Nevadas.
Worked them without mercy;
never gave up a nickel or an hour
to strikers, but starved them
off the picket line
and even put down a tong skirmish,
arriving at Promontory Point
seven years ahead of schedule.
(You try that).

In those days, men with money and ideas
got their hands dirty. Leland Stanford,
once the Big Four focused on the San Joaquin,
explored the Valley himself
like Jed Smith, Pathfinder Fremont,
or Audubon fils,
staking out the Southern Pacific route.
The only actual attorney among them,
he'd come West
after losing his law books in a fire
and opened a general store.
Governor of California during the war,
he kept the state Union.

And now, nobody's fool,
noticing the flood debris, bypassed
cow town Bakersfield to the east,
crossed the Kern
on a high timber trestle bridge,
and laid tracks a mile from
where I sit scribbling tonight,
listening to a freight train
hoot insults behind Fr. Garces' back.

Soon the SP had its octopus tentacles
wrapped around everyone
in a love-hate relationship.
The business plan:
Sell land along the tracks cheap
to lure eager farmers,
cattle and sheep men, fruit growers;
then gouge them on short haul rates
to ship their goods to market—
no choice
since that was still less costly
than wagons pulled by hay-burners.

(And yet—bottom line:
no SP,
no nothing).

LA had to be the terminus, of course,
so on and up the steep Tehachapis
where Tejon Ranch livestock grazed
at irrational angles
and teamsters still followed ancient footpaths
over the pass to the Mojave.

3k Cantonese with picks and shovels,
wheelbarrows to move tons of
blasted granite—a slow grind
up a 2% grade from the valley floor.
Loafers in town mocked them
with one foot propped on a brass rail
and a beer in their fist,
but those unstoppable stick figures drank
tepid tea from whiskey barrels,
consumed veggies by the wagon load,
amazing the beef eaters,
and kept climbing.

Hundreds buried near Caliente, the base camp,
due to vagaries of dynamite or cave ins
when half-dug, nervous tunnels
lost their resolve.
Stout ropes broke more easily than those men.

Eighteen tunnels, ten bridges,
horse shoes and serpentine S curves
and the Loop—that spiral
rail fans still make pilgrimages to see
where long freights cross themselves:
a blasting powder masterpiece, land art
more enduring than anything by Christo.

In only two years, trains grumbled
into Tehachapi, or where it soon would be,
on that single track (and still do),
slaking their thirst at the water towers.

Then more spikes driven
down to the Mojave and south
through the mile-long Newhall tunnel
and out into San Fernando Valley,
then LA—not much to boast about back then,
before the Southern Pacific…

Above the lucrative filth of oilfields
outside McKittrick, I've noticed
a gravestone on a hilltop, solitary,
enclosed by rusted iron railings.
Whose?
Should scramble up and look—
pay homage, respecting
whoever chose such a burial site
that says so much to and about
anyone who cherishes the San Joaquin.

But knee-high foxtails discourage me
along with the bull that could be up there,
temperamental as an old, alcoholic roustabout
brooding over a life lost to the rigs,
mean and if not crazy,
two fingers short of a full hand.

Down near the main road, a tar pit
gurgles amid the trash it attracts,
beer cans and dead birds
beneath torn netting—a futile gesture.

Yokuts used asphalt from seeps
to caulk their reed boats;
early white settlers marked sheep, greased,
waterproofed with it and later,
ambitious, began to process the muck for sale,
forming marginal start-ups
to dig shallow wells by hand.
More oil then than market for it.

North a few miles, McKittrick,
what's left of an early 1900s oil boom town:
scattered houses and double-wides
belonging to people who live there for
their own, indiscernible reasons;
a tavern, maybe two,
a debilitated hotel with ghost signs;
and one of those Chinese stores
that show up in every backwater on earth
and have for hundreds of years.
The owner keeps an eye on
the roughnecks buying after work beer,
some quick to pocket a candy bar
just because; on her cook, a girl
with a tramp stamp dripping grease;
and all the while chitchats
on a cell phone with her sister in Guanzhou.

Time relishes tableaus like that…

You could pan for gold in a creek bottom
(clear cold water, crisp air and pine scent)
and fry bacon and eggs in the same pan;
with minimal carpentry skills,
you could nail together a sluice box
and process much more plain sand
in a long, wasted day.

But it took funding to wildcat.
You couldn't dig in the backyard
like a child, expecting China
before nap time,
but you could spud in
somewhere among the tumbleweeds
(vile water, scorching heat and dust),
find green oil at 200 feet,
and produce ten gallons per day
drawn to the surface by a windmill.

North of Bakersfield along the Kern,
someone hand-augured into the bluffs
and filled four whiskey barrels with oil
that sold for a dollar each
as skid grease. (Now look:
an insane zigzag scribble of pipes,
tanks, plumes of steam,
and those tame rocking horse pumps
men ride all the way to the bank).

Or you could get serious
if a risk-taker puts up the money,
import drillers with know-how
from Pennsylvania, learning from them
to discern the mystical signs
of oil
and become more of a dowser
than one of those geologists dressed in khaki,
red-eyed and whiskery, never home.
Could build rigs like the Eiffel,
string drill sections together that bore
thousands of feet through solid rock
you now interpret like a seer
and bring up enough profit every day
(once the machine age has created a market)
to make your children worthless.

Which would lure boomers worldwide,
1849 all over again in 1903,
a crazed drilling rush until a man could leap
derrick to derrick
from Sunset to Lost Hills to Devil's Den—
the wells that thick for fifty miles.

And sometimes, you could get really lucky—
or unlucky—hold
a ridiculous lottery ticket that ruins your life,
a white elephant in the guise of black gold,
and bring in the gusher
at Lakeview.

Blew like Vesuvius, like Krakatoa,
toothpicked the derrick, crushed the motor shed,
flicked machinery half a mile,
and left a crater where the rig floor had been.
Men scattered instantly, black as reverse roaches
panicked by darkness at noon;
and ran as hard from glowing stones
heaved up all night.
The roar could shatter eardrums.
Oil poured down gulches into the low flats,
formed lakes men poled across in a skiff—
so much oil it glutted the market,
saturated prices
until even legendary tool pushers
had to find work in town.

Tourists rode spur line railroads out to see it,
listen to it, smell it—
that love-it-or-hate-it petro effluvium.
A preacher mounted a wagon bed, ranting
apocalypse and got thoughtful nods;
proclaimed that oil
was never intended for mankind:
it was God's holy fuel for hellfire.

Over a year like that, hopeless,
no chance of capping it,
an eco nightmare worse than the Gulf Spill.
And then the earth relented,
slowed down the flow and let men imagine
they had everything under control.

Morning

Watchman, tell us of the night,
What the signs of promise are.

That Old Clubfoot has come home,
stumping back to his non-lair
somewhere here in the museum—
an unused office, a storeroom,
a shadowed corner light never reaches,
not even at noon.

Bear-trapped as a cub, he gnawed off
most of his right forepaw
to escape
the death grip of steel jaws;
lived to prey on sheep and cattle,
or a man, maybe—
a bounty hunter
stalking that renegade grizzly,
who vanished without a trace,
except for his .50 cal rifle
and scat nearby
with a piece of plaid flannel in it.
No evidence of struggle
because Clubfoot was too quick,
though crippled, dead silent
slipping through the thickest brush,
and killed even a bull
with a single, back-cracking swat.

(We have a trap on display,
rusted half-open
with its trigger depressed like a tongue
behind a perfect set of teeth
as if just about to speak—
to express remorse
or rationalize its inquisitional cruelty.
A long ghost chain coils around it).

Sighted for decades
from Walker Basin to Tejon Pass
sometimes on the same day:
a phantom skulking in the marshes,
a boulder high on a slope
that suddenly rolled uphill into the trees.
Then nothing for months, years,
until a Basque sheepherder found a lost ewe
picked clean in the bloodied snowfall
of her own scattered wool.
Until a farmer came up short in the pig pen
and found prints in the mud—
that unmistakable, mutilated paw
leaving a pallor on his face
that made his wife ask what was wrong.
"Clubfoot."
"Where are the children?"

I've never seen him, though,
but hear him in the dark—
that faint huff, asthmatic,
that scuffing shuffle
with an odd, rhythmic claw click.

And smell him:
fetid meat on his breath,
berry juice fermenting on his chin,
the musk of hundred year old fur
like a coat discovered in a trunk in the attic,
intensely redolent of Time.
A complex aroma,
both repellent and compelling.
You can't help breathing it in
so that your precognitive senses
can decode it into
fear, fascination, foreboding.

Once some men came face to face with him
along a narrow trail
between rock and a steep drop.
Lifted his ponderous, swaying head
to sniff at them,
milky-eyed and almost blind.
Muzzle stippled with gray.
Teeth stained, you'd think by
campfire coffee and tobacco.

Just stood there
as we all hope to do
if we somehow survive like that,
outlive our own legend of ourselves.

No attack; no retreat.

Armed, the men could have put him under
like a firing squad,
but turned back, they said,
and let him be.

*Watchman, tell us of the night,
What the signs of promise are.*

That Gov. Burnett has been chiseled
from the lintel
of an elementary school named for him
and no one objected. A no brainer.
Not as if he'd been a beloved team mascot
and the activists too finely tuned,
quick as blue stockings to take offense.
Common sense in this case, not PC,
for school custodians to remove his plaster bust,
toss a tarp over it,
hide it in the back of their tool shed,
and never admit it existed
with its shameless arrogance,
thin hair like asbestos fiber
combed across a cauldron skull
seething with hatred; bitter little eyes
and that self-obsessed Brando pout.

California's first civilian governor,
poster boy for Asian exclusion,
for flogging Blacks every six months
until they moved out;
who believed exterminating vermin redskins
was sound public policy.

Why not scalp females
and skewer inhuman infants?

That even then, exceptions ruled:
a starving child offered by a withered old warrior
for a blanket was taken in and raised;
an immigrant who came across a widow
after the Whiskey Flat killings in '63
married her and raised her baby as his own,
along with their own offspring.

That everyone can do everything now—
a possibility, at least
to wear braids and a garish turquoise belt buckle
while citing obscure precedent
before the judge, a woman
whose grandfather laid tracks for the SP,
whose father owned a prosperous laundry;
to practice medicine, diagnosing
with the accent (more or less impenetrable)
of one of sixty local languages;
to be the son of someone illegal
who crawled across Sonora to get here,
and retire from the KCSD
with stars on your collar
and red service stripes from wrist to elbow;
possible to be an accountant
whose family Haggin and Carr imported
as cotton pickers.
You could run this town,
show up dapper for wine and cheese tastings,
and boast of your Okie blood
like a Mayflower snob…

The full moon has slid on its oblique
from upper left to lower right corner
of the high windows
and is gone. Its light,
the light I write by,
pools across the desktop, dull,
having lost its inward glow
along with the feeling
that it might at any moment
rise in a numinous cloud
and lift me with it.
No.
Just an ordinary moon going down.

The rattlesnake in the drawer stirs,
uncoils slowly in my mind,
and I imagine
its tongue flick, sensing
a qualitative change in the light
it will never see.

And the last coffee from the thermos tonight
—this morning—
is tepid but too weak to be bitter;
I'll drink it without tasting,
an unthinking reflex of old habits.
The mug hasn't been washed with soap
so far this year, its stains indelible
as bad memories
that only darken if you try to scour them.

Besides, here on the night watch
where I determine the superstitions,
it's unlucky to clean a coffee mug,
and grunge heals like penicillium mold.

And the wooden pencil I write with,
a dawdler best suited to rumination,
is too soft and slow for a world
where dozens of insect texts
can skitter back and forth before
I fumble illegibly
to the far end of this sentence
with all its false starts, scratch outs, addenda,
and lines tossed to the margins to lasso
a stray metaphor.

And the leaves of this legal pad
have become jaundiced:
they've heard it all before and then some;
would refuse the imprint of graphite
if they had a choice. The words
crawl across their skin like flies,
stubborn, determined not to be brushed off.
It must be maddening.
No.
Just writing paper, inanimate
unless you consider the life in wood—
thousands of trees pulped continually
for our sins, sacrificed
so that we can scribble redemption
all night long. Tell me:

Do you lean down over the paper and hear
the ghostly, Mississippi accent
of wind in the loblolly pines?
Do you?
I promise not to scoff…

Tall, stooped, his face less wrinkled
than crumpled—Lincolnesque,
bearing an excessive human burden,
he paces the floor,
not dressed in black with a stove pipe hat,
but wearing cowboy drag—
a fifties country musician
in a white satin shirt with gold piping,
gold fringe, and sequined red roses;
slacks to match and
shimmering saddle-tan high-heeled boots
doodled with white stitches.

Scrapes a fiddle clamped under his chin
while he talks, lock jawed:
"Didn't think you'd make it through the night
without me, did you?"

No comment.

"Remember when you were on your own
too late in life for your own good?"
And sings in a round, pleasant baritone,
"Looking for love in all the wrong places."

Every night, he comes with something new—
an endless songbook of recrimination.

"An old girl came on to you
one night in Trout's.
The wreck you said
must have pawned her teeth
and either lost the ticket
or never could raise the cash to redeem them."

Yes.
Skin the color of overripe plantains
with the texture of jerky
and stuck to her bones like papier maché
on a wire frame.

"A lush you looked down on
—somehow—
from the deep hole you were in,
so hard up she spoke to you.
And what did you do?"

"You tell me."

"Skedaddled like a lizard
under the nearest rock.
That was back before you dried out
and got religion. So—
feel any better about yourself?"

Another no comment.

"And how about my grandson?
You recognized him from the old neighborhood
when he panhandled you on the street;
had that *help me* look in his eyes—
just about to glaze over
and give up.
And what did you offer
a week before the OD killed him?
A gospel tract and three dollars?
Or was it just
a weak grin as you wished him well, hoping
he could keep warm and well fed?

"Think about it, old-timer."
He saws an angry screech
that rips him to tatters,
vanishes in a satin fluttering...

Watchman, tell us of the night,
What the signs of promise are.

That nevertheless, passing Time in the past,
assuming its familiar local colors,
helps keep your own past at a safe distance.
Sometimes. Maybe.

That these ghosts, friend or foe,
indifferent or sneering,
stalking like the puma upstairs,
or keeping to themselves
like the Yokuts in their village behind glass,
whose baskets overflow
with enough troubles of their own;
these ghosts at least entertain me:
their curses as well as blessings
occupy the solitude
that could consume me otherwise.

And not everything past is hard to take,
is it? Even the fiddler
brings back a soused Saturday night
after the Pumpkin Center Barn Dance—
that vast, double-wide Quonset hut
with plain lettering on the façade
and just as unadorned inside.

The car a packed circus clown act
of musicians who'd drunk
more than they earned, again—
the righteous fiddler among them,
and others a decade from undreamed of
fame: names you know.
Me stuffed underfoot on the floorboard,
looking up at them (still do),
trapped, close to claustrophobic panic,
hours beyond my bed time.
My parents blithering up above in the jumble.

I think that was the night
Dad kept grabbing someone's anointed Stetson,
noli me tangere,
and got tossed out of the backseat
into roadside rose bushes—
and shredded.

Watchman, tell us of the night,
What the signs of promise are.

That Time will make peace with me,
settle the old grudges, bury the has-beens,
if I'll go with the Heraclitian flow—
the Kern River
I was thrown into at birth
to bob like a cork until I learned to swim,
believing for years that my stroke
was so strong I could swim upstream
if I wanted. Now
the rocks are too slippery to hold onto;
the undertow is reaching up for me
and, sooner or later,
I'll have to let go—let go
and let that glad roar explain everything,
that madly exhilarating churn
of white water
wrap its angelic arms around me,
irresistibly, and take me home…

Last rounds.

No custodial duties anymore.
Drunk drivers in orange vests
take out the trash and sweep once a week,
sentenced by a judge
to community service that used to be my job.

Soon the museum director will arrive,
turn her toothless old key in the Yale lock
and accept the imperatives
of her own desk,
sorting the dayshift paperwork—
invoices, requisitions, another memo
from the County Board of Supervisors
reminding her to cut the budget,
beginning with the useless night watchman.
Memos she has ignored.
So far.

Now the very last, feeble moonlight,
the light I've written by,
lays a friendly hand on my shoulder,
right where the ache is, and whispers,
"There's nothing more you need to say,
believe me."

The insect husks on display, empty
and ignored like pill bottles
on the nightstand
next to a bed where someone has died;
domesticated wildflowers
with something like botanical dementia,
their labels faded,
complex Latin names illegible;
my own life preserved
only by memory's amateur taxidermy
so that these stuffed animals,
birds and mammals,
must still be alive somehow—
or I'm not.

Blind glass eyes, recognize me.

Upstairs, the puma growls softly
—gently?—
no more threatening now
than the air conditioner's hum.

Sunlight outside the high windows
waits to clock on and go to work.
Still in no hurry.
The ghosts have all gone back to their day jobs
as bookkeepers for oblivion
or docents in the endless museums
of the past. And the night watchman?

The night watchman has left the building.

Notes

Night Watch

I've known the night watchman since we were in kindergarten together at Roosevelt School. When he handed me this ms to read and asked for comments, I suggested he might append notes to clarify some of the local references. He groaned. Like most "scribblers," he doesn't think explanations are necessary, that poetry simply means what it says. But when I offered to help out, he shrugged without saying either yes or no. I took that for a yes.
  -editor

    The poem takes place in the mind of a night watchman during a single shift in the Kern County Museum, which both is and is not the former institution.
    The museum building itself still stands on the north side of Bakersfield between the Kern River and the vanished Blackboard, that notorious honky tonk where legendary country musicians used to dodge beer bottles, at least in my timid imagination. Originally, the collection was housed in a corner of the Chamber of Commerce Building—a large and appealing structure, something like a no-nonsense California mission if its faith had been business. It opened in 1929, a month before the Wall Street Crash. Over the years the museum exhibits expanded until they finally forced the chamber out. Not long ago, however, the museum finally gave up; the structure, returned to its original interior, is now a rental venue for events. Sad for the night watchman and his ghosts, who no doubt still haunt the place, confused by the changes.
    Next to the museum is the reconstructed Beale Memorial Clock Tower that occupied an intersection downtown until the 1952 earthquake deconstructed it. Behind it lies Pioneer Village, likely the most irenic place in Bakersfield, shady and parklike, its streets lined with relocated historic homes and businesses. The original fairgrounds is on the other side of the museum, separated from it by the Black Gold exhibit. Behind that is the problematic

Sam Lynn Ball Park, named after the longtime Coca Cola distributor. Here dream-blinded young men still have to bat their way out of the minors facing into a fierce afternoon sun.

The interior of the museum depicted on these pages is no more or less actual than anything else. We visited it now and then from childhood on, including that elementary school field trip to sit in bleacher seats in a sunlit room and watch a Yokut woman weave a basket, which my old friend has written about.

"That and everything else I see in my mind is vivid—perhaps too vivid to be fact. But as always, it's a question of form and shadow," the night watchman says. "And who's to say which is which."

p11 *Kern County.* Oil and Ag. Comprises a large chunk of central California, a couple of hours north of LA. Bisected by the Tehachapi Mountains (Southern Sierra Nevada) with the Mojave to the east and the San Joaquin Valley to the west. 8k square miles shaped like a sheet of paper in landscape orientation with its left side torn off along a ragged edge. This is where the Joads landed and where the space shuttles came to earth. True locals like the night watchman, the son of Midwestern refugees, have Dust Bowl bona fides. *Grapes of Wrath* was burned here and still smoldered when he was a boy.

p11 *three in the morning.* Actually not quite one. The night watchman is thinking of Scott Fitzgerald's comment in *The Crack Up*, "…in a real dark night of the soul, it is always three o'clock in the morning."

p12 *Granite Station.* A stagecoach stop in the foothills where horses were changed, hard liquor consumed, and lies told no doubt (as they are told in these pages). The families who grazed cattle in the area when the station was established in the mid 1870s remain there today. Somehow the roadhouse didn't burn down until 1993. For the night watchman, the place is the center of the earth, and he still goes there occasionally to gaze out over the valley beyond the charred chimney.

p15 *Tehachapi*. A mountain community halfway between the Valley and the Mojave that developed around the Southern Pacific depot built there in the 1870s. The name may be an Indian word for "steep climb"—appropriate since the railroad grade includes the Loop where long freight trains cross over themselves as they struggle up into the mountains. The center of the '52 earthquake, which leveled the original town.

p15 *the wind to feed on*. See the opening lines of Villon's *Legacy*.

p16 *Wheeler Ridge*. The area near the foot of the Grapevine where I5 enters the south end of the Valley. Along with his vague memories of poppies growing from the shoulder of old Hwy. 99 all the way to the foothills, the night watchman once saw an issue of *National Geographic* from the thirties with photos of fields even thicker than in his own childhood.

p18 *Weill's Department Store*. Alphonse Weill, a teenaged French immigrant, began as a clerk in a general store, opened his own business, and saw it grow into a full blown department store. His family managed it until like so many institutions and landmarks it was done in by the earthquake. That any of its manikins ended up in the county museum is another of the night watchman's unlikely confabulations.

p19 *Yokuts*. The indigenous people who occupied the entire San Joaquin Valley and the western slopes of the Sierra Nevada Mountains. The foothill tribes were wiped out during the Gold Rush; those in the Valley dwindled away due to the white man's diseases and cultural shock. Hunters and gatherers and fishers with a reputation for peacefulness, mostly, their surviving baskets are highly collectable and astonishing works of art. One tribe operates a casino these days.

p22 *improv history*. Historians are advised to take the night watchman seriously on this point.

p22 *Pioneer Mercantile.* The last of the old school hardware stores, it opened in 1889 and hung on until 2012, finally forced out of business by big box stores where the help wanders around as helplessly as the customers. This clerk obviously took pride in knowing his stock.

Reclamation

p25 *Kern River.* Rises from snowmelt and small lakes somewhere west of Mt. Whitney and would descend—if left to its own devices—over 150 miles to its ultimate dead end at the southwest corner of the San Joaquin Valley in the Buena Vista Lake bottom. This lake was always seasonal and often dry, but even after the reclamation projects of the late 19th century, the river would occasionally flood the Bakersfield area;,1893 was one of the worst years.

    For this reason, and to regulate water (the true gold) for essential irrigation, the U.S. Army Corps of Engineers constructed the earthen Isabella Dam in the early fifties, creating Lake Isabella with Old Kernville beneath it. In 2006, its keepers discovered that the dam had begun to seep; since then, it has been maintained below its capacity—just in case. If the dam were to fail, Bakersfield would go under within a few hours.

    Below the dam, the river takes its course along a fault line, also a potential danger here in earthquake country. But that's just a possibility we live with; the real danger of the lower Kern, the "Killer Kern," is drowning in its treacherous waters. A sign at the mouth of the canyon warns us—in English and Spanish—to stay out and stay alive. A no brainer. Unless you're drunk or, as most locals believe, a foolish outsider from southern California who scoffs at the sign and opts to wade in one of those quiet pools with sinister undercurrents. The count of the drowned is now over 250 and will inevitably increase. *Cavete flumen.*

p26 *Road's End Lodge.* I knew it as Pasco's Lodge, a restaurant and store with many green cabins beneath the trees. Cool and breezy, the river tumbling below. In the summer of 2002, a campfire got away from someone and burned for six weeks, destroying almost 17k acres and most of the available buildings, including the old lodge. As so often happens, the fire spared three cabins for no discernable reason. The night watchmen likes to imagine that one was the cabin he stayed in as a boy.

p28 *Old Kernville.* Now beneath Lake Isabella, except during the driest drought years when foundations appear as the water recedes. After the government had claimed the land behind the dam-to-be, the buildings were moved to higher ground (the present day Kernville), torn down—or dynamited, which would at least add some fun to a sad affair since there's nothing more entertaining than blowing things up.

p28 *Movie Street.* Old Kernville had a decidedly wild west vibe, so part of it was kept that way intentionally—the street unpaved, the old flat storefronts left intact as the town modernized with asphalt, gas stations, and neon signs outside the cafes. Many westerns were filmed there and in the nearby canyons and deserts. I've read that the set was hauled to Barstow or somewhere and used for bombing practice during WWII. But who knows. The night watchman is convinced that he remembers Movie Street.

p29 *Lovely's Big Blue.* In 1860, a Cherokee miner named Lovely Rogers picked up a rock to throw at a runaway mule and discovered gold in his hand. A lovely tale, but the mine was fact, yielding $12 million before it finally closed in 1942.

p29 *Whiskey Flat.* Since alcohol wasn't allowed at the mine, an entrepreneur went down by the river and set up a board-and-barrel saloon, calling the place Whiskey Flat. A town grew up around it, soon requiring a more suitable name. Kernville honored Fremont's cartographer on the expedition that had passed through the Kern River Valley in 1845, mapping the river and some of the county also named for Edward Kern.

p33 *kept to the mountain towns.* Where there was gold or rumors of gold while the valley seemed uninhabitable due to floods and malaria. Quartz ledges discovered by Richard Keyes in 1854 led to the first rush into the area. About ten years later came the discovery near Havilah ("where there is gold" Gen. 2:12). Which became the original county seat until that function was transferred to Bakersfield, the valley proving viable after all.

p33 *Christian Bohna.* The first white man to establish residence where Bakersfield would come to be. Born in Germany in 1805, he apprenticed as a blacksmith and then immigrated to New York to escape family drama. From there, he kept moving west as men with wanderlust did as long as there was a frontier. He used up a couple of wives along the way, fathering close to a dozen children who still have descendents in Kern County. Bohna returned here from Oregon and, like Baker, died in 1872.

p35 *but exhaling dust.* "The air was thick and stale as if it had been breathed in and exhaled again as dust." Charlotte Jay, *The Fugitive Eye.*

p35 *Col. Thomas Baker.* Really did have an alfalfa field that he opened to travelers gratis as an opportunity to promote the town he dreamed of. Along with being a world-class booster, Baker was a self-taught lawyer, militia officer, businessman, former state legislator, surveyor and construction engineer. Born in Ohio in 1810, the grandson of a Revolutionary War vet, Baker came West following the Gold Rush and gradually drifted south and inland from the bay area. Along with Bohna's modest holdings, Baker picked up a huge reclamation franchise, no doubt at a deep discount, and soon set to work. He died during a typhoid epidemic in 1872 and was buried in the cemetery he had only recently established for the community.

p35 *They call their lands.* Psalm 49:11

p37 *even hiring some.* Baker employed three dozen Indians from the Sebastian Reservation as the work crew to dig his canals.

p37 *as scripture tells us.* The night watchman is somewhat misconstruing Prov. 21:1.

p38 *one ton plow.* Unfortunately, it didn't quite work, demonstrating once more that bigger isn't always better. It seems the oxen moved too slowly to cast the dirt to the side and so it fell back into the ditch. The Souther Plow is here on the museum grounds somewhere, still brooding over its failure.

p38 *Chinese labor.* Used throughout the West for construction of the infrastructure that made prosperity possible, building everything from these canals to the railroad that crossed the Sierra Nevada. Even more expendable than the Irish, who themselves had less cash value than Black slaves.

p38 *Kern Island Canal.* Bakersfield was originally known as Kern Island because it set on high ground above the swamp. This canal does continue to flow through the city, though much of it is underground. The other canals, ditches, and drains still exist as well, those listed lying primarily in the west side of the county. Main Drain Road north of Buttonwillow follows the sinuous course of the canal so closely across flat land that you can easily get car sick driving it as if you were on a winding mountain road.

p39 *the witch.* Every neighborhood had one. The night watchman insists this incident actually happened and hasn't been embellished. But—consider the source.

p40 *an empty river.* By the time the Kern passes through Bakersfield, its water has been drained off by canals. That upriver users take most and leave a trickle for those downriver is a conflict in the history of irrigation that dates back to ancient Egypt. After lawsuits and deals galore, the river remains dry except in the wettest years, and if not for Isabella Dam's problems, there would never be water in it. Local ironists have marketed tee shirts with the slogan: A riverbed runs through it.

Wanderlust

p41 *traffic that runs circles.* Sooner rather than later, every growing community must reroute the highway that overlaps its main drag. So Bakersfield sent Hwy 99 on an end run (off tackle, actually) that came back across Chester Ave. at the north end of town. The solution for dealing with combined traffic at that point was the Garces Traffic Circle. Adequate then, but subsequently a tricky and dangerous roundabout characterized by the unruliness of Rome rather than an orderly ebb and flow. No one can risk a glance at the statue that rises from the small island. This 1935 WPA commission was carried out by the Finnish sculptor, John Palo-Kangas, who didn't know Garces from those beefy heroes of the working class he had carved elsewhere. He also did the statue of Thomas Baker outside the city hall, which comes closer to a likeness of its subject.

p41 *the plywood box.* An overpass was built in the early fifties, sending the increasingly heavy highway traffic above the surface streets. This required moving the statue of Garces from the center of the circle to the southern edge, where he stands today. In the fall of 2009, the overpass was upgraded, a project lasting two years or so. Rather than moving the statue, a wooden shelter was built to protect it during construction. This fact would tend to date the text to the late summer of 2010, perhaps on August 24 when the moon was full. However, that is merely a fact: the night watchman seems to be writing at an earlier period.

p41 *Fray Francisco Garces.* One of the amazing mystic wanderers of the American frontier who ought to be legendary. He entered the Franciscan order as a teenager, his calling to the priesthood blended with an unquenchable romantic thirst for far places. Too restless to sit tight and administer his assigned missions in the southwest, Garces spent as much time as possible away from the office, exploring, discovering, and evangelizing the indigenous peoples. He was often alone or accompanied by a few local guides, but never by troops with supplies. Indians took to him, protecting him from each other or passing the word ahead that the solitary priest was a stand-up guy. In the end, of course, that didn't help. Only 43, he was killed in 1781 by Yuma warriors who had had it with white men, period—slain because of what he was, despite who he was. Not unusual in human affairs. Second white man into the San Joaquin, a couple of years after Don Pedro Fages (note follows), he was first to cross the Kern River.

p41 *Mojave was his wash pot.* Psalm 108:9

p43 *an ancient sea floor.* The San Joaquin, covering central California between the Sierra Nevada and various coastal ranges from Sacramento south to the Tehachapi Mountains. It was indeed a Miocene sea teeming with marine life, much of which ended in the Shark Hill fossil deposits outside Bakersfield when the ocean dried up due to earthquakes sealing the San Francisco Bay, silting, and other geological whimsies.

p43 *foul air.* Bakersfield always ranks high (low?) among cities with the worst air in the U.S. Locals refuse to accept the blame, however, insisting that the pollution flows south from the bay area and other northern cities until it hits the dead end of the valley here. Some new residents who arrive midyear have actually had no clue that the town is surrounded by mountains until one January morning after a rain when they look around and gasp in wonder.

p43 *Don Pedro Fages.* A Catalonian officer who was briefly in charge of all Spanish forces in Alta California until the arrival of Portola. He was in fact searching for deserters when he entered the San Joaquin Valley by way of Grapevine Canyon in 1772, earning bragging rights as the first white man of record to do so. An effective commander and skilled bureaucrat, he was nevertheless outmaneuvered by Father Junipero Serra, founder of the California missions, and lost his job. He made a come back, though, and had an outstanding career until shortly before his death in 1794. If he wasn't as anti-clerical as the night watchman portrays him, he had every reason to be. His wife was a diva, and the couple could have been the subject of California's first reality show along with their other firsts.

p46 *Buena Vista.* The wanderings of the Kern River ultimately ended in the Buena Vista Lake basin. But even then in the wettest years, the river kept moving, following sloughs north into other seasonal lakebeds. Buena Vista survived until the completion of the Isabella Dam left it low and dry once and for all. Not quite. A manmade lake now covers a portion of its original area. On any summer weekend you can find it by simply following a pick-up towing a ski boat that is heading southwest out of Bakersfield. No doubt it's on its way to Lake Webb.

p46 *decorated by Joshua trees.* In his journal, Fages misidentifies the distinctive Joshua trees of the Mojave as palms.

p48 *Pauline itch.* Rom. 15:20.

p49 *like beetles.* The retired priest is alluding to Wittgenstein's famous thought experiment, Beetle in a Box (qv).

p50 *ace of spades.* In cartomancy, always bad news: emotional conflict, obsession, death or at least a bad outcome.

p50 *and Him crucified.* 1Cor. 2:2.

p51 *El Rio de San Felipe.* Garces' name for the river; later changed by another priest-explorer to La Porciuncula after the abandoned chapel in Assisi restored by St. Francis as the home of his order; finally called the Kern by John C. Fremont in honor of his topographer, Edward Kern.

p53 *wading across.* Garces was piggybacked across the river on May 1, 1776, not far below the mouth of the canyon.

p53 *Bear Mountain.* Breckenridge Mountain, next door, is much more impressive at 7500 feet compared to this hill's mere 2000. Breckenridge also features giant Sequoias on top—a short if miserably contorted drive from the valley floor. Up there Time (using the capital T as my friend would) scrambles Indian mortar rocks with the transmitter towers of local tv stations. Nevertheless, Bear Mountain, although it offers only a snobbish gated community on its eastern slope, attracts the eye to its rounded summit at the southeast corner of the San Joaquin and has always been, along with Granite Station, one of the night watchman's sacred places.

p54 *Pascal's wager.* Essentially, that if you believe in God, and he doesn't exist, you've lost nothing; but if you reject Him, and he does exist… Sorry about your luck.

p54 *St. Phillip's Ethiopian eunuch.* Acts 8:36

Pilgrims

p57 *Pilgrims.* A name for immigrants going west, but specifically applied by trappers to anyone new to the fur trade. Though pejorative, the tone could vary from amusement to contempt. Best known, of course, as a marker for bad John Wayne impressions, along with "little missy." But the night watchman uses it more generously and more generally: We are all pilgrims, some with better survival skills than others, but all half lost most of the time, searching for that illusive low pass through the high mountains.

p57 *The new Ford caught fire.* When the night watchman and I are sipping wine from the 805 and need to get our minds off the horrors of this world by considering its weirdness, one of us always brings up this fire. Vinyl siding? Who knew—and, as they say, surreal. We came upon the aftermath while driving around randomly one Sunday afternoon. The condos are located a block or two from the site of Alexis Godey's house in Bakersfield.

p58 *Alexis Godey.* That fame is a lottery is the only explanation for his relative obscurity compared to other mountain men, Jim Bridger or Kit Carson, for instance. Godey did it all. The night watchman has merely cherry-picked a long career that could be—and has been—the subject of an entire book.

p58 *Rio Bravo.* Yet another early name for the Kern, commonly used by Mexican settlers. Now familiar as the name of a mega-ranch, country club, and a run of class II white water not far from where Garces crossed the river.

p58 *Tejon Ranch.* Your basic empire. Gen. Edward F. Beale—a player nationally as well as in Kern County, notably as Superintendent of Indian Affairs—put it together in the '60s from four original Spanish land grants and some public land, operating as a sheep and cattle ranch. When his son sold out to a syndicate in 1912, the *LA Times* characterized the holdings as the size of Rhode Island. It was ultimately incorporated in the mid-thirties and thrives to this day—diversified, even marketing a line of high-end, expensive sport shirts with a little Tejon Ranch label on the pocket. The night watchman covets one. Meanwhile, a surviving band of Yokuts lives somewhere out there (they say), well-secluded, with no public access allowed.

p59 *full moon.* Once more, this corresponds with August 24, 2010.

p60 *Jedediah Smith.* Definitely cut from different cloth than other mountain men—a preacher's black rather than buckskin. But no less rugged or more hesitant to kill, if it came to that, despite his devout Methodist faith. More intelligent than his comrades, he was consequently more ambitious. His ultimate goal was to map terra incognita and publish his journals—like his original inspiration, the journals of Lewis and Clark. Certain Comanches had another agenda. Discovered South Pass, the principal immigrant trail into Oregon country. In this case, "discovered" means that he talked the Crows into telling him where it was. First American overland into California, passed north through present day Kern County in February, 1827.

p63 *Biddle edition.* After Lewis' (mysterious) death, Nicholas Biddle took over the project preparing the journals for publication, along with Paul Allen. The Biddle-Allen Edition appeared in two volumes in 1814 when Jed Smith was a teen. He may have kept his copies his whole life.

p63 *possibles bag.* The personal possessions of trappers were known as possibles.

p64 *dead last son.* Younger sons or outcasts of the British upper classes, known as "remittance men," weren't rare in the West. They were paid to stay far away; but this son has nothing coming and isn't getting a quid.

p64 *midday sun.* Alludes to Noel Coward's famous lyric, "Mad dogs and Englishmen stay out in the midday sun."

p65 *Ft. Vancouver.* A year or two old at this time, the northwest headquarters of the Hudson Bay Company. From there, trapping parties went far beyond their assigned boundaries, even reaching the south end of the San Joaquin Valley.

p65 *Ft. Ross.* Russian outpost on the Mendocino coast, established in 1812 and mostly thrived until 1842. Once the region had been trapped out and the California missions secularized, cutting off agricultural supplies, it was abandoned.

p65 *foofarow.* Still in the dictionary, but familiar mountain man slang. We'd say: bling.

p66 *gone beaver.* To go under is to die; gone beaver is dead and buried—hopefully; otherwise you became wolf meat. Like Jed Smith.

p67 *Fremont.* Not to mention innumerable other accomplishments and controversies, California governor and US senator, he owned the vast Las Mariposas cattle ranch in the northern San Joaquin; also owned much of the old San Emigdio land grant south of Bakersfield, though he never visited it. Fremont made and lost a fortune and more reputations than almost anyone else on the frontier. And he had the ego for it. He and his wife were radical abolitionists, cutting edge Republicans. In our time, Jessie, his devoted publicist, might have made the better presidential candidate. Perhaps an even more remarkable personality than the Pathfinder himself, she died in LA in 1902.

p68 *Percy Shelley.* The night watchman is at it again. Having earlier compared Col. Baker with Poe, he now claims to notice a similarity between Shelley and an a portrait of the young Jessie.

p68 *lean bull, fat cow.* Mountain man slang for hard times and good times.

p68 *stiffed an old Yokut.* In *The Flock,* Mary Austin relates the complaint of this man that he had worked hard to rig a ferry so that Fremont's party could cross the rampaging Kern and received nothing for his troubles.

p69 *Carson.* Although a dime novel cliché, he more than earned his legendary status. Cherubic in looks and young, Carson trapped with Ewing Young in the southern San Joaquin. Soon respected, a man's man, he could have barely made the limit for a Disneyland ride, though estimates of his height vary. An illiterate squaw man who spoke a half dozen native American languages plus Spanish.

p69 *Walker.* Poster child for Manifest Destiny. Went to war in 1812 as a horse boy in Andy Jackson's command; fought the Red Sticks with Sam Houston; hired by Bonneville to lead trapping expeditions into the far west. Deeply involved in the US home invasion of California through the back door of the Sierra Nevadas. Walker Pass connects the Mojave Desert with the Kern River Valley. Hwy 178 still follows the original trail, continuing from Kernville down the river and on into Bakersfield.

p69 *that pit.* Yosemite is a perfect example of why the elderly shake their heads sadly and say, "I've lived too long."

p71 *Kern.* Fremont had a gift for recruiting the best, men such as Carson and Godey among others—and Edward Kern. Not only did he sketch and map the entire West—and his maps were works of art—he did the same throughout Asia with the US Navy. All of this and he died of an epileptic seizure at the age of thirty nine. He ought to be honored by more than the name of a county that gets no respect.

p71 *Lebeck.* The epitaph carved in an oak, mentioned in several early journals, was finally overgrown by new bark. But when someone broke off chunks, it reappeared on them as raised letters in reverse. Lebec (as more commonly spelled) remains mysterious, perhaps the most enduring local legend. The carved bark can be seen in the visitor center of the Ft. Tejon State Park. The night watchman believes that he saw it as a boy on display in the old county library before the earthquake. But his memory is notoriously inventive.

p71 *Ol' Ephraim.* Mountain man slang for grizzly bear.

p72 *Audubon.* Led a large party up from Mexico into California and on to the San Joaquin in 1848 to study birds and wildlife, continuing the work of his father.

p73 *Peg Leg Smith.* A Kentucky mountain boy who ran away from home citing abuse. But he must have been a handful. Followed the righteous Smith's route into California and up the San Joaquin in 1830 where he organized Indians around Tulare Lake into a band of horse thieves preying on the coastal missions. He camped along the Kern while driving stolen horses east to the Santa Fe market.

Beginners

p75 *Beginners.* I read somewhere once that Jedediah Smith, though certainly not a hater, considered the Indians to be a transitional life form between animal and human. An odd proto-Darwinian notion for a Christian, which might make them something like novice people—beginners. Certainly most whites anticipated the social Darwinism that emerged toward the end of the century, believing indigenous cultures to be less than fully developed, that is, still at the beginning stages. I suspect the night watchman's title intends to mock that attitude while also using the word in its other sense: those who begin something; you could even say *founders*, couldn't you? At any rate, the night watchman would never use a contemporary locution such as First Peoples, which would set what's left of his teeth on edge.

p75 *the local snake man.* Everyone who attended school in Kern County from postwar to the nineties witnessed one of Al Robbins' presentations. Ultimately, when a PC helicopter mom complained about potential danger (how times have changed), Fish and Game raided him, confiscated his snakes, and shut him down. But Robbins had so much juice (venom?) in the community that the government agents had to back off and return his snakes, coming up with some way to issue him the necessary permits. Not the case with the Chinese immigrant who lost his farm for plowing under a kangaroo rat. No one had ever heard of him.

p76 *beginner's mind.* In Shunryu Suzuki's classic, *Zen Mind, Beginner's Mind,* the premise is (roughly) that we can maintain spontaneous enjoyment of life in the face of routine and drudgery only by keeping the attitude of a beginner, for whom everything is fresh and possibilities are unlimited. Perhaps the basket weaver, in exchange for the peace she gives the students, is blessed by seeing her own work through their eyes, always for the first time.

p78 *the basket weaver.* The night watchman's breathless account is reminiscent of those images of the Virgin appearing in a rust stain or a tree stump. Surely it can't have been anything other than an ordinary field trip; I don't even remember it. But he insists on his memories and refuses to back down. It is a fact, however, that a Miss Trout taught third grade at Roosevelt School in the early fifties.

p79 *Woilo.* The principal village of the Yowlumne sub tribe of the Yokuts, whose territory extended from the Grapevine Canyon in the south well up the Kern River.

p80 *Harvey House.* Begun in the late 70s, Fred Harvey's chain of restaurants serving Santa Fe passengers provided for the first time to travelers both edible food and polite service. The "Harvey Girls," known for clean fingernails and good morals, did offer an upscale alternative to the run of unattached women on the frontier. Opened in Bakersfield circa 1900. Early fire maps of the town show many properties identified with the euphemism, "female boarding," most of them conveniently located next to a saloon.

p81 *breaking his teeth.* Acorn flour was ground with stone mortars and pestles, and grit was unavoidable. Yokut teeth were chipped and worn down over time.

p83 *Indian casinos.* There are none in Kern County—yet—although a couple are an hour or so away and are popular destinations. A local tribe has received the legal status that will make such a venture possible. Pearl Stud is a hater, of course, but most people look on the lucrative casinos as a kind of reparations program, preferable to government handouts. However, whenever billions of dollars are involved along with a lack of accountability and secrecy made possible by Native American sovereignty, controversy and the potential for corruption are inevitable.

p85 *Diggers.* Probably the ugliest derogatory term for Central California Indians. Based on their root gathering, but a response, really, to these people after the depredations of white society had left the survivors resembling today's street people.

p85 *slip of paper.* Leaving theological issues aside, Pearl Stud has inappropriately quoted Jer. 48:10, Isa. 13:16, and the blood chilling Psalm 137:6.

p90 *his report.* This episode is derived from the Keyesville Massacre of April 19, 1863, in which soldiers of Easy Company, 2nd Cav. along with local volunteers tallied a body count of thirty five. The victims had most likely slipped into the Kern River Valley from the eastern slopes of the Sierras where the Inyo War was heating up. Capt. McLaughlin's report makes the points included here, even the sticks and stones.
Mishmash

When Native American tribes are hiring anthropologists to teach them their own culture and bringing in linguists to recover their lost language, you know the Melting Pot has boiled dry. The idea here is *diversity*, but of course the night watchman refuses to use that word. He has chosen something more apt, if messier. His own ethnicity consists of ¼ German blood and the rest whatever it is that comes down from the North Carolina hills.

p92 *Woolgrowers.* Bakersfield is known for Basque restaurants. This one was a hole-in-the-wall when I was a child and my earliest memory of going out to eat. I even liked the pickled tongue. Incredibly, Barbra Streisand and her husband used to eat there when they passed this way.

p92 *Charles Ives.* When we were in our twenties, the night watchman used to drive me nuts by making me listen to Ives' music before he got over that enthusiasm. American as transcendental apple pie, haunting and lyrical at times, though wildly experimental. One of his pieces, for instance, recreates the sound of two marching bands approaching playing different tunes, passing through each other and then on into the distance.

p93 *apocryphal tunnels.* Sober-minded Chinese commentators insist there never were any tunnels under Chinatown, only passages connecting cellars or large basements of commercial buildings broken up into individual storage units that gave the appearance of tunnels. But that's no fun.

p94 *satanic cult.* Any discussion of the Chinatown tunnels segues into rumors about the secret underground chambers all over Bakersfield (most of us could point out a couple of houses that supposedly have them) and from there, inevitably, on to the "Lords of Bakersfield" (qv, if somehow you've never heard of them).

p94 *highbinders.* Gangsters in 19th century Chinatowns.

p95 *Say Yup kid.* Despite the property ownership restrictions, repressive legislation, and the herding of all Chinese into a few square blocks of town while limiting them to certain occupations (big money was made in the laundry business in the long run), many immigrants did well and their offspring even better—literally the American Dream. Ming Yen is known not only for his large, successful farm and produce business along with numerous good works on behalf of the Chinese community, but for his death. Two hours after his wife died, Ming was gone too, thus achieving a rare "Butterfly Marriage" in which the couple mate for life and die simultaneously. Say Yup was his home province.

p95 *Gum Shan.* Gold Mountain, originally California during the Gold Rush.

p96 *eminent cattle family.* The renowned J. J. Lopez was the eldest of sixteen siblings born into a California family that had produced a hundred years of outstanding cattlemen and administrators. Doctor's orders moved him from the indoor to the outdoor branch of the family, first with sheep and then cattle. Gen. Beale hired him and before long he was running the Tejon Ranch livestock operations. The corporate owners who took over in 1912 brought him out of recent retirement to run things once more; after his second retirement, the indispensable Lopez continued as a consultant until his death in 1938.

p97 *Tiburcio Vasquez.* With Joaquin Murrieta, the most famous of California's politico-outlaws, as alluring to many people as Che himself. The night watchman is not among them. Though active primarily in the north, Vasquez moved into the southern San Joaquin when the heat was on. No doubt passed through Bakersfield on his way to or from the LA via the Tejon Pass.

p98 *Hispanic surnames.* Ruiz, Eldeo, Ensinas, Maron, and the boy, Elias—a significant lynching by any standards. The white Yoakum brothers, accused of ambushing someone over a mining claim dispute, may have had the clout to get away with it. They fought the mob so viciously that one of them had to be shot and strung up dead. Otherwise, there were few lynchings in Kern County: a Black man at Mojave and Yung Fook somewhere up on Breckinridge.

p99 *Tevis...* Truxton Beale, the son of the general, inheritor of Tejon Ranch (which he sold ultimately). Haggin and Tevis, following a protracted court battle with California land barons Miller and Lux, whose downstream river water they had drained off, incorporated as the Kern County Land Company. And there you have the big three of the southern San Joaquin.

p99 *Gen. Beale's camels.* Originally Beale's notion, agreed to by Jefferson Davis, then Sec. of War, camels were imported and used for many purposes, including a cavalry unit. However, nothing seemed to work out for a number of reasons: muleskinners couldn't relate to them, the climate wasn't quite right, the Civil War intervened, and so on. Beale did train a pair to pull his buggy from the ranch to LA in good time.

p100 *second-hand store.* Owned by E.W. Winters, the business was lucrative for many years. Members of one of the first Black families in Bakersfield, the Pinkneys, owned the saloon, one block from the center of town, which seems to have thrived until Prohibition.

p101 *off limits.* By city ordinance, Chinese were allowed to own property only within the set limits of Chinatown, as mentioned above. Ming's holding were, of course, well south of town.

p101 *Butternut county.* Refers to the color of Confederate uniforms and, by extension, supporters of the southern cause. Kern County has always been and, to a degree, continues to have a southern vibe—Nashville West. Due to the large number of Confederate sympathizers during the build-up to the Civil War, troops were stationed at Visalia and Fort Tejon, which had been closed a few years earlier. It has been suggested that if California had been admitted to the Union as a slave state, the San Joaquin Valley would have been cotton plantation country.

p102 *daddy's Cadillac.* Something like a local version of the Baroness de Koenigswarter's Bebop Bentley in New York City (qv).

p103 *Chinese cemetery.* Not absorbed by the housing boom until the mid-fifties. I remember trucks being loaded with red steel drums to be relocated—who knows where. Upscale houses were then built around a cul-de-sac, and when the swimming pools were excavated, even more skeletal remains appeared with an even less certain dispensation.

p104 *hard things.* Overheard remark. The night watchman was tasting in a winery on the central coast that had a rusted Radio Flyer as part of its décor. When an older customer commented on how rough the ride was and how often he had crashed in his wagon, the young man who was pouring the wine kept up the long tradition of bartender-philosopher, saying deadpan, "That's how we learn that hard things hurt."

p104 *joss house.* The original Chinese temple was built of wood in a strawberry patch, just up the street from the current, small brick structure (1890s) on or near Alexis Godey's land where the former Coca Cola bottling plant building still stands. "Guailo" is Cantonese, derogatory slang for Caucasian—literally "white ghost." The patriarch of the family that owns the Mexican restaurant got his start in business with money saved from earnings as a railroad construction worker—like Ming Yen.

True Crime

p105 *Chalifoux.* Jean Baptiste may have left home as early as the age of thirteen to join the fur trade, but no one really knows much about him until he appears as a trapper based at Taos. In 1837, he organized a large band for the purpose of acquiring horses in California—not strictly illegal since it wasn't a U.S. possession. Yet. He passed through the southern end of the San Joaquin Valley on his way home, driving a herd too large and noticeable not to attract others in the business of acquiring horses. The etymology of Chauganosos remains vague.

p107 *John Mason.* Both he and his partner were recruited by a Confederate sympathizer with money who wanted to organize a force of partisans in California, something along the line of Quantrill's Raiders in Bloody Kansas. Nothing much is known about Mason prior to this, but Jim Henry already had a record from criminal activities in the Mother Lode. In appearance, a Mutt and Jeff team, they were equally unconscionable, though they liked to call themselves Confederate soldiers. No one was fooled.

p107 *Copperhead.* Strictly, a member of Vallandigham's northern peace party, but commonly applied to a southern sympathizer in a Union state. Also Butternut (cf note for p62).

p108 *Philo Jewett.* The Jewett brothers, Solomon and Philo, introduced Merino sheep to Kern County and went on to play a major role as developers, not only in agriculture, but in oil and railroads. Established the Kern Valley Bank, the first in Bakersfield.

p111 *Robber's Roost.* A rock formation on the eastern slope of the southern Sierra Nevada Mountains. Its caves and crevices offered varied hiding places, and the view overlooked miles of desert, including the road from the Cerro Gordo mining district (which operated into the mid 1950s) and the Walker Pass Road into the San Joaquin Valley. Both routes were used to ship ore and valuable supplies; both were frequented by stagecoaches whose passengers carried all sorts of interesting plunder.

p114 *Peter Singer.* Moral philosopher for whom human beings simply exist, without intrinsic purpose or value. Every ethical choice becomes: it depends (qv, if that appeals to you).

p115 *fan qui.* Foreign devils (i.e. Caucasians).

p115 *coolie.* Racial slur for Chinese day laborers.

p116 *Kunming.* Where the night watchman's father was stationed in WWII, along with other outposts in the CBI (China-Burma-

India Theater). Originally the base for the Flying Tigers, later for the intrepid C46 pilots who flew cargo from India over the Hump.

p116 *moves a mountain.* From the *Analects,* attributed to Confucius.

p118 *devil.* "…Christians do not paint the devil on the wall." – Kierkegaard

p118 *er hu.* Chinese stringed instrument with a drum-like sounding box, played upright. Imagine a cross between a banjo and a cello that sounds like homesick bees.

p118 *hatchet man from the tongs.* Chinese benevolent associations were formed for mutual assistance all over the West, much like the Odd Fellows who had halls in every town. Inevitably some drifted into the vices for the money to support their programs; others were started by men with ties to organized crime at home. Hatchet Men (boo how doy) were hired mercenaries who engaged in the protection racket in the manner of Mafioso and took care of enforcement. Tong wars were sometimes fought over these interests into the 1920s, ultimately being staged for Chinatown tourists a la Deadwood and the OK Corral.

p118 *wrapped around their heads.* So that enemies couldn't get a grip on their queues in a fight.

p120 *Jim McKinney.* A decent kid gone bad due to alcohol, the wrong friends, and loose women—so they say. But he went farther to the dark side than a typical mean drunk would go without a natural tendency toward it. Robbed, killed, and ran amuck all over the West and Mexico from his home base in Kern County. In the aftermath, shocked locals began to get serious about cleaning up the vice along with the horse manure in the streets. It is said that twelve year old Earl Warren, future Chief Justice, was among the lookie-loos after the smoke cleared. His own father was later murdered in the family home in East Bakersfield; the case has never been solved. The joss house remained unchanged until wrecked by the earthquake of 1952.

p120 *piano player.* "Don't Shoot the Piano Player," Francois Truffaut's 1960 New Wave film.

p120 *R brain.* Or Reptilian brain, the basal ganglia which, in MacLean's evolutionary model, is the oldest part of the brain and responsible for instinctive behavior, aggression, and dominance.

p120 *Al.* Jennie Fox went her way, but Al Hulse, who survived the shootout, was convicted of murder and sentenced to life—in the county jail. No surprise he committed suicide some years later, slitting his own throat.

p120 *Winchester dogs.* In hatchet man parlance, rifles and pistols were known as dogs and puppies. Hence the order to open fire: Let the dogs bark.

p121 *the son.* Town Marshall Jeff Packard died in the shootout along with his deputy, Bill Tibbet. His son Lawrence Tibbet, seven at the time, went on to develop one of the outstanding operatic voices of his era. Also successful as a radio personality and actor with an Oscar nomination for a lost Laurel and Hardy film.

Empire

p122 *160 of wheat.* If a farmer could develop his operation until he owned the four horses required to work 160 acres, he had achieved critical mass. Pioneers survived, sort of, with basically Neolithic techniques. On the other hand were (and are) the mega ag businesses such as Frank Norris describes in *Octopus* (below): thirty plows behind three hundred horses cultivating literally miles of land, arrayed in the V formation of migratory birds.

p123 *plows forged at an ironworks.* Innovations in equipment were essential to farm vast acreages in the San Joaquin, and not all of those new devices originated in the Midwest. Beginning by fastening three plows side-by-side and increasing the horse power needed to pull them, valley farmers ultimately perfected the Stockton Gang Plow, which was used by wheat growers worldwide. Improved seeders, cultivators, combines and other sophisticated tools also came from central California.

p124 *steam tractor.* One of Oliver Hyde's Overland Steamers arrived in Bakersfield in 1875, leased for a few months by W.B. Carr, who was growing wheat galore. Billy Carr was Haggin's partner (below) during the great water litigation several years later.

p125 *Haggin.* James Ben Ali Haggin, a Kentucky lawyer with a Turkish mother, along with all of his other enterprises both in California and nationally, owned a half-million acres of this county. With his partner, Lloyd Tevis, he ultimately formed the massive Kern County Land Company. Tevis built a mansion on the outskirts of Bakersfield, which he never lived in, that became the local country club. The original home burned down, however, before the golf course opened. The Stockdale Country Club is surrounded by the city now, although it was still a long bike ride into the sticks when the night watchman and I used to pedal out there occasionally.

p125 *Lux v. Haggin.* Water law is Byzantine in its complexities and more vicious in practice than Barbary Coast piracy. The case went on for years, stifled the economy of the county, and set precedents that still stand. This is no place to attempt an explanation of the issues. Haggin's partner at the time, W.B. Carr, was squeezed out before the formation of Kern County Land. Henry Miller, his opponent, actually assisted Haggin in the construction of weirs and reservoirs after the settlement—a gracious man by the standards of the era. It is also said that a hobo could receive a meal and a bunk at any of Miller's ranches.

p126 *Saroyan.* Fresno's William Saroyan was the night watchman's first favorite author, for whom he still has admiration despite Saroyan's collapse in the literary ratings. Sort of like a first love, perhaps. No one has ever evoked growing up in the San Joaquin like he does, Armenian or otherwise, according to my old friend. But I'd have to mention Gary Soto and, for the land itself, William Everson (qv).

p127 *Generic.* There are a few men he might be—even a local or two, given some hyperbole in the description. But presumably RB stands for Robber Baron.

p130 *friend.* Me. Among the subjects we've discussed over a bottle of wine from the 805 is that school year in China, not long before Tiananmen Square.

p131 *Huntington...* The Big Four need no introduction. Interesting, though, that all were native upstate New Yorkers who migrated to the Midwest and on to California—their spiritual homeland—during the Gold Rush, though they wasted no time on their knees with a pan. None had formal education. All were hands-on businessmen (hardware, groceries, mercantile) who built their enterprises from near scratch to filthy lucre before turning to visionary levels of finance, politics, and empire building. They all owned mansions on Knob Hill in San Francisco. All four were abolitionist Republicans. And they had lives apart from legends to live. Stanford's only son died young, in whose memory the university was established. Uncle Mark Hopkins died inconceivably in testate without heirs, leading to the subsequent soap opera of his widow's remaining years. Huntington ended an invalid, never recovering from injuries suffered in a carriage wreck. And Crocker—the huge monument above his grave on a hill in Oakland is a blatant, unembarrassed phallus.

p132 *cooked the books.* The Credit Mobilier scandal broke in 1872 and got ugly on a national level, involving even the presidential election. Basically, to offset their enormous risk in a railroad across the continent that wouldn't make money on operations for years to come, the clever lads of the Union Pacific established their own construction company, ostensibly independent of the UP. Then they overcharged the government for construction costs, pocketing the excess through various laundering techniques involving buying and selling bonds. Or something like that. Mark

Hopkins apparently tossed the ledgers into the incinerator to protect his partners.

p132 *Judah.* Theodore "Crazy" Judah is more proof that money matters. Although he dreamed the impossible dream of a transcontinental railroad, proved it could be done (on paper), and sold the concept the Big Four, they forced him out of the conglomerate. Easy. Just up the ante until Judah couldn't afford to stay in the game. Died young of yellow fever contracted while crossing the Isthmus of Panama on his way to NY to attempt to raise capital.

p134 *octopus tentacles.* Muckraker Frank Norris' 1901 novel deals with conflict between wheat growers and the railroad, based on the SP, that ends with the gunfight at Mussel Slough (1880). *Octopus* is one of those famous novels everyone alludes to but few actually read. As a metaphor, it has entered into cultural literacy and needs no elaboration.

p135 *the Loop.* The rails laid from the valley to Tehachapi summit remain one of the great accomplishments of railroading and are still the longest single track in the nation. The route had been surveyed in the 1850s by army engineers assigned by Secretary of War, Jefferson Davis. But it took blood, sweat, and genius to construct it. The man behind the project was William Hood, Dartmouth '67, who went to work for the Big Four immediately after graduation and retired fifty one years later as chief engineer of the SP. The famous Loop makes its full circle at Tunnel 9, about half way up the grade. Visible from Hwy 58, it's a treat even for old guys to see an 85 car freight train snaking over its own tail.

p135 *Christo.* His 1340 huge yellow metal umbrellas were installed in the Tejon Pass in 1991, complimented by even more blue umbrellas in Japan. The project was dismantled in September of that year after one of the yellow umbrellas toppled and killed a spectator.

p138 *hand-augured.* The Elwoods, father and son, drilled this little well, followed quickly by another more commercial well—and then thousands. The Kern River field has over 9000 active wells, the third largest field in California. It has produced close to a billion barrels on the outskirts of Bakersfield, creating an eyesore from the Panorama Bluffs—unless you have oil stock or can enjoy the glittering lights at night without thinking about what they are.

p139 *Lakeview.* The famous/infamous Lakeview Gusher blew in the spring of 1910. It flowed without letup for almost eighteen months, producing over nine million barrels. One hundred years later, the Gulf Oil Spill lasted for a couple of months and released about five million barrels of oil.

Morning

p141 *Watchman.* Lines from a Victorian hymn by John Bowring used by Charles Ives for one of his vocal pieces (no. 70) as well as appearing occasionally elsewhere in his work, including the 4th Symphony.

> Watchman, tell us of the night,
> What the signs of promise are.
> Traveler, o'er yon mountain's height
> See that glory-beaming star.

p141 *Clubfoot.* This legendary grizzly with the same back story appears throughout the West. Often, I suspect, more fact than fancy since bears mutilated by a trap were not all that rare. The most well-known Clubfoot was finally shot in the Oregon-California border region in 1890, stuffed, and mounted on a wagon for display as far away as the Chicago Exposition of '93. Ultimately disappeared, perhaps a victim of the San Francisco fire following the earthquake of 1906. The Kern County Clubfoot was last seen around 1879.

p144 *Gov. Burnett.* Peter Burnett, the first civilian governor of California. He had previously served as a legislator in the Oregon territory, pushing through racial exclusion laws that included the flogging mentioned here. That law remained on the books until 1926. Burnett was so frustrated by resistance to his leadership style and policies that he resigned after a year in office. His racism was extreme, but not unusual for his time. He anticipated the Asian exclusion laws that became national policy in 1882. Many—though by no means all (see below)—shared his good-equals-dead attitude toward the indigenous tribes. In a speech to the state legislature he proclaimed that "a war of extermination will continue to be waged between the races until the Indian has become extinct." The elementary school in the Hunter's Point neighborhood has been renamed for Leola Havard, the first Black woman principal of a San Francisco school.

p144 *bust.* The night watchman's invention. However, I've googled Burnett's photograph and that is indeed the classic Marlon Brando pout.

p145 *exceptions.* The pioneer Rankin family, still thriving in Walker Basin, has passed down the story of taking in a starving girl, part of Capt. Moses McLaughlin's exodus of a thousand or so Monache Indians through Walker Pass and down into the Valley to the Sebastian Reservation on Tejon Ranch land. In another family story, German miner Fred Butterbredt married the widowed "Betty." Descendants still live in the Tehachapi area.

p145 *KCSD.* Kern County Sheriffs Department.

p147 *grunge heals.* The night watchman is at least half serious about his theory that old coffee-stained cups possess healing properties.

p148 *fifties country musician.* The fiddler is someone actual, not invented, but the night watchman won't allow me to identify him. The incident with the grandson is one of those occasions in life when you could easily have done the right thing, but didn't. It remains something my old friend regrets.

p148 *"looking for love."* Song by Wanda Mallette with Bob Morrison and Patti Ryan. A hit recording by Johnny Lee, it was featured in the soundtrack of *Urban Cowboy*.

p149 *Trout's*. Second in legendary status only to the Blackboard, a country music venue for as long as anyone can remember and still open. Others that deserve mention in the same breath with these two honky tonks: The Lucky Spot, Rainbow Gardens, Beardsley Ballroom, and the dance hall below.

p150 *warm and well fed.* James 2:16.

p151 *Pumpkin Center Barn Dance.* Located in a wide spot in the road south of Bakersfield known by that name, the austere but ample warehouse offered no frills, just serious local country musicians, many soon to become famous, and plenty of room to dance. Something of a family activity, though, because children were admitted (as the night watchman well remembers and old photos verify). Other than the name painted in plain black letters, it featured one modest neon sign perpendicular to the building with the word DANCE.

p152 *anointed Stetson.* According to a cherished family story, the hat belonged to Buck Owens and remained firmly on his head.

p152 *Noli me tangere.* Do not touch me. Spoken by the resurrected Jesus to Mary Magdelene in the Vulgate (John 20:17). Also said to have been inscribed on collars around the necks of deer owned by Caesar: "Noli me tangere, Caesaris sum." Which is closer to the way it's used here, of course.

Note on sources: When I asked the night watchman if he used Wikipedia like the rest of us, who pretend we don't, he didn't deny it. "Mostly memories and imagination," he said. "Good guesses and shameless lies. Otherwise, I browsed through whatever was lying around the house." On his shelves, I came across the following volumes: Wallace Morgan's fascinating *History of Kern County, California* (1914); an earlier edition of *Garden of the Sun* by Wallace Smith; *Inside Historic Kern* published from its quarterly by the Kern County Historical Society; an excellent summary pamphlet from the Title Insurance and Trust Company, *The Story of Kern County*; *Historic Kern County* by well-known regional historian, Chris Brewer (a descendant of Thomas Baker); the delightful low-budget, spiral bound *Old Bakersfield: Sites and Landmarks, 1875-1915* by Lynn Hay Rudy, also with deep roots in the community; Camille Gavin and Kathy Leverett's *Kern's Movers and Shakers* with its succinct but detailed biographical entries; the wonderful oral history, *The Chinese of Kern County 1857-1960* compiled from the papers of the late historian emeritus, Harland Boyd; and finally I noticed among others by the indispensable Gerald Haslam, *The Great Central Valley* and *Workin' Man Blues: Country Music in California.*

Photo by Chris Thompson

About the Author

Like both the night watchman and the editor, the two voices of *Local Color*, Don Thompson is a native of Bakersfield, California, and has lived in the southern San Joaquin Valley for most of his life. He began publishing poetry in the early sixties, producing a number of books and chapbooks over the years. *Back Roads: A Journal* won the 2008 Sunken Garden Poetry Prize. Most of his work interacts with the landscape of the Valley, but in *Local Color* he turns to the history of the region, to the people as well as the place. Thompson and his wife, Chris, live on her family's farm— land once owned by Miller and Lux, who reclaimed it, and before that, of course, by the Yokut, who hunted and fished the original wetlands.

www.ingramcontent.com/pod-product-compliance
Lightning Source LLC
Chambersburg PA
CBHW062218080426
42734CB00010B/1934